T0348918

FULL OUT

FULL OUT

LESSONS IN LIFE AND LEADERSHIP

FROM AMERICA'S FAVORITE COACH

MONICA ALDAMA

G

GALLERY BOOKS

NEW YORK   LONDON   TORONTO   SYDNEY   NEW DELHI

Gallery Books
An Imprint of Simon & Schuster, Inc.
1230 Avenue of the Americas
New York, NY 10020

First Gallery Books hardcover edition January 2022

GALLERY BOOKS and colophon are registered trademarks of Simon & Schuster, Inc.

For information about special discounts for bulk purchases, please contact Simon & Schuster Special Sales at 1-866-506-1949 or business@simonandschuster.com.

The Simon & Schuster Speakers Bureau can bring authors to your live event. For more information or to book an event, contact the Simon & Schuster Speakers Bureau at 1-866-248-3049 or visit our website at www.simonspeakers.com.

Interior design by Jaime Putorti

Manufactured in the United States of America

10 9 8 7 6 5 4 3 2 1

Library of Congress Cataloging-in-Publication Data

Names: Aldama, Monica, 1970– author.
Title: Full out : lessons in life and leadership from America's favorite coach / Monica Aldama.
Description: New York : Gallery Books, [2021]
Identifiers: LCCN 2021003030 (print) | LCCN 2021003031 (ebook) | ISBN 9781982165918 (Hardcover) | ISBN 9781982165932 (eBook)
Subjects: LCSH: Aldama, Monica, 1970– | Cheerleading—Coaching. | Women coaches (Athletics)—United States—Biography. | Personal coaching. | Conduct of life.
Classification: LCC LB3635 .A38 2021 (print) | LCC LB3635 (ebook) | DDC 791.6/4—dc23
LC record available at https://lccn.loc.gov/2021003030
LC ebook record available at https://lccn.loc.gov/2021003031

ISBN 978-1-9821-6591-8
ISBN 978-1-9821-6593-2 (ebook)

Dedicated to everyone
who stays after practice to clean up

CONTENTS

CONTENTS

FULL OUT

INTRODUCTION

GO FULL OUT!

One fall afternoon in 2017, my daughter's boyfriend was at our house watching a show about junior college football in the living room. I walked by and was instantly sucked in. Once I sat down and started watching, I couldn't look away. It was only a couple of weeks after that that I received an email from someone named Omar Bustos saying that he was one of the producers of that same documentary series (called *Last Chance U*) and that he was interested in speaking to me about doing a show about cheerleading.

Is this some kind of prank? I thought. *A scam email?* I actually wondered if he had some way of seeing my Netflix queue and knew that I had been watching *Last Chance U*. Not to mention, if this was legit, I had mixed feelings about the prospect. I'm a very private person. I don't like to be watched. But I had also been frustrated for a long time about cheerleading not being taken seriously. This would be an opportunity to show the world what cheerleaders really do. I was willing to throw my fears out the window if it meant getting more respect for the sport.

I told him, "If you're looking for some kind of *Dance Moms* story, I'm afraid you won't find that here. I'm not going to do any fake yelling. I'm not going to give you some kind of made-up drama. But I do want people to know how serious this sport is."

I went and talked to my athletic director about it. We thought it was worth investigating, which eventually led to a conference call that included Greg Whiteley, who was not only the director but also the creator.

To me, Greg has the good looks of someone you might think was from Los Angeles, but he's not flashy or slick—he has a kind and quiet demeanor. He's the kind of person who makes you feel like you've been friends forever. And I found I was inspired by the way he talked about filmmaking. He told me he tried to film "with a cold eye, but a warm heart." I had a gut instinct about Greg: he was a good guy.

He said he wanted to get an authentic story but would always be mindful of people's feelings and explained that with a documentary, the crew isn't there to make the story good or bad. Whatever the story is the story is, that's what they have to relay. Any crew could get amazing footage of the tumbling, he said; he took that for granted. But what he thought his crew could do differently was find the very best stories and tell them well. I hung up thinking I wanted to watch the show, whoever he wound up making it about. But when it came to Navarro College, where I coach, I thought, *There is no way this will pan out*. I assumed Greg was talking to a lot of cheer teams, and it seemed unlikely that he would pick one in Corsicana, Texas.

But then he did pick us. He and a small crew came out in February 2018, and they filmed us practicing for a couple of days and put together what's called a "proof of concept." Netflix bought it and the rest is history.

When the show got the green light, Greg called me and said they were going to come in and film twelve hours a day for about four months, and that whatever they got was what they got. They were going to tell a true story. I hoped it would show people how hard cheerleading is: the athleticism, the grit, the hours that we put in. I felt like it was worth taking the risk to put our story out there so that everyone could see what we actually do.

It was good that my instincts about Greg were right, because from the time he and his crew started shooting, they were here with us every single day. They weren't just at practice; they were also following us around when we left the gym. Soon we were telling them everything about our lives—they became part of our family.

Since the Netflix documentary *Cheer* introduced America to the cheer program in my Texas town, I've heard about people adopting the mantras of cheer life—rules like, "Always catch your teammates," or, "Practice until you can't get it wrong," or, "Cheer for your team even if you're not the one 'on mat.'" And I saw one story calling me "the Bill Belichick of cheerleading, if Bill Belichick had perfect square French Tips." Look, I'll take it.

My life as a successful coach in a small town was as much a surprise to me as it was to everyone else. When I graduated college more than twenty-five years ago, the big city was calling my name. I wanted the excitement and the hustle and bustle of someplace like New York City, even though I'd never even been there.

But let me back up. The story of who I am as a coach and how I work with my team really starts way before the job opportunity presented itself. So much of how I work my team is an outgrowth of things I picked up along the way.

I was born in Alabama and moved to Corsicana, Texas, a town of roughly twenty-five thousand, when I was six years old. I started first grade in Corsicana and graduated high school here, then earned a finance degree at the University of Texas at Austin. After graduating, I married my high school sweetheart, Chris. We're both "fly by the seat of your pants"–type people. In typical fashion, we got an apartment in Dallas before either of us even had a job. As a result, I took the first position I was offered—sales manager at a computer company. Though it paid the bills, it was a grind.

A year in, one of my high school friends called me about a job back in Corsicana at Navarro College. He told me that the cheer coach was leaving and that I should apply because he remembered how much fun I'd had cheering for his mother when she was my high school cheer coach. At this point, I still had Wall Street in the back of my mind, but Chris and I didn't have the money to make that move yet. And even though I'd spent years dreaming of moving to the big city, I also knew that I wanted to have children soon. Being near family in Corsicana had its appeal. I hadn't gotten a lot of time with my own grandparents; I wanted my children to know theirs.

I figured this could be a temporary stepping-stone to my dreams in the business world. I applied and got the job. So began my journey—twenty-six years and counting—of learning, failing, succeeding, and growing in the world of cheerleading.

When a film crew started following us around a couple of years ago I didn't think much of it. I thought the cheer community might watch the documentary. Actually, I *hoped* the cheer community would watch, but I had no idea what to expect. Then it came out and became one of the biggest docuseries of all time. We went on the *Today* show, *Oprah*, and *Ellen*. Quizzes appeared online with titles like "Which *Cheer* cheerleader are you?"

Cheer itself caught me completely off guard. I've watched it four times now and cried every single time. I love my kids with my whole heart. While I knew the outlines of their lives, there was something about seeing where they grew up and their families that made me understand how they fought to get where they are now.

I also realized that coaching such diverse groups of young people to fourteen National Cheerleaders Association junior college division national championships has taught me what makes a team work. These lessons apply to every situation in which leadership is important—in the workplace, in parenting, and really in everything difficult we ever try to do in life. I love that people who have never even done a cartwheel (and trust me, at age forty-eight, it's been a while for me, too!) are now well versed in terms like *mat talk, basket toss*, and, of course, *full out.*

Full out means a full run of a routine from start to finish with all skills executed. But to me, it also means much more than that. Going full out means approaching life with courage and commitment. You give everything to the task at hand and leave it all on the field. People who live life full out push through exhaustion and insecurity in the interest of doing their absolute best and supporting those around them—teammates, bosses, family, and friends. Again and again, I've seen young people in my program apply what they learn in the gym to other areas of their lives with amazing results.

Since the show came out, I've gotten requests from people of all ages, asking for advice or life-coaching. At first it surprised me. But I think everyone, including me, struggles with the balance between having compassion and high expectations for ourselves and others—and not just in athletics. We're all training for our own versions of the National Cheerleader Association College Nationals in Daytona.

In this book, I'll share what I know about goal-setting and achievement as they apply not just to cheerleading but to all aspects of work and home: how a $5 planner can change your life, the power of positive self-talk, and why you can learn everything you need for success from how to build a successful pyramid.

Whatever your field, the same principles should rule your team: trust, hard work, discipline, community, consistency. There's a lot of talk these days about shortcuts and life hacks, but I don't think we focus enough on values like integrity, doing your best even when you're not getting the glory, helping your friends, and improving together with your teammates.

Cheer is so much more than girls with pom-poms. What these men and women do is physically grueling and psychologically intense. Your teammates push you to be the best, call you out when you're slacking, and pick you up when you fall. Without stamina, organization, and the support of your community, not only will you not succeed, you will get yourself and others hurt. The stakes in cheerleading are no joke.

We all continually work to be the best versions of ourselves. What is your Daytona? And how can the lessons of cheer coaching get you there? I'll share the secrets of finding inspiration, staying motivated, and getting the best out of people (including yourself). We all need someone cheering for us. With this book, I am cheering for you!

1

DISCIPLINE IS A GIFT

I stroll into the Navarro College gymnasium expecting to find my cheerleaders on the mat stretching and getting ready for practice. They'll be wearing color-coordinated shirts, with the color indicating which day it is, drinking water out of water bottles given to them by the trainer, and chatting. Only on this day, I walk in and find them yelling, screaming, and collapsing into piles.

Someone who didn't know better might think that it was a brawl. But I know what they're doing, because I've seen it oh so many times before: they are reenacting an episode of *Bad Girls Club*—an Oxygen reality show about seven rowdy women sharing a house in L.A. It's many of the kids' favorite show and they love to act it out in the most realistic way.

On this particular day, some of my cheerleaders are playing Bad Girls. They're pulling one another's hair and pretending to have meltdowns all over the mat, running as if they're wearing six-inch heels and holding back their make-believe long hair. Others are pretending to be security guards keeping the others from killing one another.

I stop in the doorway and take it in for a minute. Then I start laughing and I can't stop. There's just something about a bunch of kids acting rowdy that feels like home to me.

I think it has a lot to do with my time in Alabama. When I moved to Texas at the age of six, my parents and I left the rest of the family back in Alabama, though I still spent every Christmas and summer there visiting my grandparents and cousins.

My grandmothers lived about a mile from each other in a pretty rural part of the county—the kind of place where people don't lock their doors—but the two women could not have been more different. My mom's mother was a feisty thing who would give you a run for your money and a cussing-out if you needed it. Once she made me pick a branch off the tree in front of her house in case she needed to give me a good ol' country whipping for not following the rules. Sending me to get the switch might just have been a scare tactic, but it absolutely worked. I never gave her cause to use it. And there was something about the discipline at my maternal grandmother's that felt oddly soothing.

My mom was the oldest in her family. From an early age, her biological father was not in her life. My grandmother eventually met and married my grandfather, who adopted my mother. Then they had five more kids. The age difference between kids was so great that my grandmother was pregnant with her youngest at the same time that my mother was pregnant with my sister, Melanie. My mom's little brother felt less like an uncle and more like a cousin because he was our age.

With three girls and three boys, my grandmother's house was pure chaos. The boys were constantly getting hurt because they were wild and rambunctious. Kids were always yelling or running through the house, or out exploring the many acres they lived on. It was nothing to have someone come in with a finger half cut off or with a fishhook stuck into a leg. The boys loved living on the edge— maybe too much.

Both my grandmothers grew their own food because they'd grown up poor, and they made every bit of soil count. My grandmother also kept pigs and chickens and was as tough as you need to be to slaughter animals and hoe fields. If we tried to push the limits a little too far, she didn't mind handling business. I have vivid memories of her wearing her muumuu-style nightgown with a cigarette in her hand, cussing at my grandfather. What a woman!

When I was only fourteen, she passed away from cervical cancer. It had spread throughout her body before they caught it. I miss the time we didn't get to have, and I regret not having her around to talk to now. My kids would have adored her; I can imagine how she would have made them laugh.

When I went to my father's mother's, my mamaw's, the difference was stark. She sang in the church choir. She was a Christian lady. Absolutely no cussing at all. She was so gentle that I could get away with anything at her house and I sure did.

Mamaw's husband, my granddaddy who I never met, had a heart attack when he was in his forties, and after that she lived quietly alone, maintaining a simple schedule. I needed more stimulation and pushed Mamaw's buttons out of boredom. On one visit, my sister, Melanie, and I decided to make pizza at 2 a.m. We woke our mamaw up with all our banging around in her kitchen. It's not that we were *bad*, necessarily. But we were loud. I'm sure after those visits in the summer Mamaw was all too ready to ship us back to Texas.

I have an aunt on my dad's side of the family whom everyone said I resembled: my aunt Jessie, the oldest of nine children. She never had kids of her own and she divorced early. I knew her as a strong single woman and successful businesswoman who traveled the world and who knew all about real estate and investments.

I found her so impressive. She never minded calling people out. If there was ever a problem, she was always the one to handle it. Problem with the condo management? Jessie was already on the phone working it out. On vacation and need a doctor? Jessie had found one before you could sneeze twice. Because of our shared habit of taking charge, I was nicknamed Little Jessie. I was honored.

I definitely have my aunt Jessie's spunky personality and direct-ness. I learned from her how to wield power and tell everybody what to do. In high school I was class officer and served on the student council, where I loved being involved in decision-making.

Maybe that's why I feel comfortable today as a coach. I don't mind disciplining those who need it, whether making them run laps or do push-ups or simply giving them a good talking-to. That's not to say I don't second-guess myself. At the end of every year I think, *What could I have done better? What could I have done differently to have been more successful in this area or that area? Or with this student?* But over the years I've gotten better at knowing when someone needs more discipline or less. Most need more.

There's a shared thread of discipline running through my whole family. In various ways, we've all found ways to create structure amid chaos.

My dad went into the air force after graduating high school. After his service, he worked for a company that refurbishes train wheels. He worked his way up to VP of operations, a job that required him to travel throughout the United States and Mexico to visit the factories. He had a powerful work ethic. He set high expectations for me, and I always wanted to live up to them. As I grew up, I looked for my dad's approval above all else.

I adore my father but he was very stern and old school. If I didn't meet his high expectations for me there was no discussion. He would just point at me and snap his fingers. That's how I knew to get in line. While corporal punishment was certainly still popular in Texas in the '70s and '80s, I really didn't get that many spankings, because the ones I did get made a lasting impression. I had great respect for my dad and I never wanted to disappoint him. I always wanted to make good grades, and I always wanted to do better and better, because I wanted to make him proud.

My mom stayed home when we were babies; then she went to college and got her teaching degree. After teaching for a year or two, she bought a day-care center, which she ran until just a couple of years ago. She was wonderful at keeping the little kids in line while keeping her composure.

My husband, Chris, has a criminal justice degree and is the director of adult probation for Navarro County. What I see in his work and in my own work is that my cussing, smoking, switch-cutting grandmother had it right: compassionate discipline is the key to creating a world in which people—whether toddlers or felons or flyers—feel free to make good choices.

The truth is, we all need to have limits imposed on us, for the good of society and for our own well-being. Young people in particular need structure. At the same time, they also need compassion. I feel blessed that I was able to grow up with both. There were rules and expectations, but I was also able to make mistakes and still know that I was loved.

2

DON'T ASSUME EVERYONE
ELSE IS LIKE YOU

To whom much is given, much will be required." That's a phrase I think about all the time. To me, it has a lot of meanings. When you're blessed, you should give back. If you're blessed financially, it's your responsibility to give to those less fortunate. If you're blessed with stability, provide a calm port to those who are at sea. If you're blessed with wisdom, help those who need words of encouragement.

I've been working with teens and young adults for almost my entire adult life. So I know that all teenagers struggle in one way or another. They do a lot of looking for approval. If you don't have structure at home and you're looking for someone or something to make you feel good about yourself, you can get caught up with the wrong crowd. Kids this age don't fully know who they are yet. It's a particularly vulnerable time: when you're looking to shore up your identity, there's always going to be someone saying, "Come over here. We'll love you, we'll accept you. All you have to do is get wasted, stop caring, drop out of school. What we do is cool."

Everyone wants to feel loved. The teenage years can be a scary time for kids. They are trying to figure out where they fit in. The people with whom they surround themselves are crucial during this time. A lot of teenagers are not strong enough yet to walk away from temptation. Their need for acceptance is intense—too overwhelming for a fragile young ego—and bad choices are made.

This is why the role of a parent is such an important one. It is part of a parent's job to guide a child and to monitor who their friends are. It is important to have open communication so they feel comfortable coming to you when they are happy or sad, and perhaps especially if they are in trouble. They have to feel they can ask for advice or have a shoulder to cry on. And they must feel safe with you; otherwise, they will hide everything and look to others for that sense of belonging.

I was raised in a typical middle-class family. Materially, I had everything that I wanted and supportive, present parents. I didn't lack for anything. I grew up in a good environment. And when I was young, I just assumed that everyone else was more or less like me.

It wasn't until I started coaching that I realized how different other people's childhoods could be. I had to look hard at my own assumptions and realize that plenty of people grow up in poverty or in abusive households. Sure, I knew that in the abstract. I watched the news. But I didn't really understand that reality until I started coaching and hearing people's stories. Over time, I realized that learning how to be a good coach meant teaching myself how to see other people for who they really were, not how I assumed them to be.

To become a good coach to all the kids, I needed to learn about where they came from and what they'd experienced. I had to find ways to relate to them and to see the world through their eyes. And I had to understand that everyone is motivated by something different.

Some kids want toughness. That's what I always craved. I don't really get my feelings hurt ever. You can be as blunt as can be with me. But I've learned that not everyone is like that. Others will crumple at the slightest correction.

Allie was much more sensitive than some of the others on the team. She didn't have any experience flying—being thrown into the air—when she came to Navarro, so we really had to start with the basics. Learning the techniques involved in college coed partner stunting can be tedious. There are many things that need to be addressed, from body positions to dismounts. We could be working simple double-downs and I'd say, "Hey, Allie, you need to point your toes a little more," and she would start crying.

"I didn't say your double-down was *bad*!" I would tell her. "I'm just trying to make it a bit better." But she would still look defeated. Sometimes I feel like coaching should require a psychology degree.

With experience, I've learned to be more strategic when I'm giving feedback. You can be very direct to one child, whereas the same approach might hurt another's self-esteem or lower their confidence.

You have to think beforehand about how you want to communicate, because once you've killed someone's confidence, you're definitely not going to get the best out of them.

One afternoon a few years ago I was hanging out with a girlfriend when she mentioned an item in the news at the time: a Corpus Christi woman had been arrested for spanking her two-year-old daughter. She was sentenced to five years of probation and mandatory parenting classes. My friend thought the woman should have gone to jail. I wasn't so sure. In my mind, physical punishment wasn't necessarily always unacceptable.

"I certainly received my fair share of spankings when I was a kid," I said to my friend. "I think I turned out okay!"

"There's a difference," she said, "between your dad giving you a whipping and some of these households where the kids live in fear."

"Oh, come on," I said. "You're exaggerating. A spanking doesn't make kids live in fear."

My friend told me that I was not being empathetic to this particular little girl's situation.

"Of course I'm being empathetic!" I said. "I'm kind. I'm a good person. I have everybody's best interests at heart!"

But that conversation really made me analyze what empathy truly means. I thought a lot about what my friend said. I realized that she was right: spanking's not the same in every home. *Nothing's* the same in every house.

I couldn't assume that just because spanking was common and even encouraged in my childhood meant it was always a good idea for everyone or that in some homes it might have a very different effect than it did in mine.

I started trying harder to put myself in others' shoes. Not long after that, I got pulled over for speeding. And at that moment, I thought, *Here's a moment where one of my Black students would probably have a very different experience.* As a middle-aged white woman, I was not even flustered. I even thought, *If I'm charming enough with this officer, maybe I won't even get a ticket.* It made me think: *If I was Black, would I be nervous, or scared, or think differently?*

Watching footage of the *Cheer* documentary, I found my understanding of the squad's challenges grow even deeper. I had known the gist of my kids' stories, but I didn't know the details. And the details were hard to hear.

Seeing their profiles in the documentary made me understand them much better, and I was glad to see how much the world responded to their spirits. It's one thing to hear, "I had it rough as a kid." It's another to hear about abuse and neglect. When you see these brave young people pouring their hearts out, how can you not feel moved?

Seeing Morgan Simianer's family story also broke my heart. She's incredibly hardworking and such a kind soul. I couldn't believe she wasn't bitter about being left to fend for herself at such a young age. I heard that members of her family didn't like the way they were portrayed on the show, but all she had revealed was that her mom left when she was little and that her dad, saying she could take care of herself, left her on her own when he remarried and had a new family. Those are just the facts. And her dad wasn't wrong: Morgan is a very capable girl. She was certainly able to feed and clothe herself. But that doesn't mean she didn't feel a deep sense of abandonment and longing for family. Bless her grandparents for taking her in and showing her the love and support she craved.

Before the show, Morgan was always trying to make sure she had enough money to pay her rent, but now she doesn't have to worry—her rent's paid. Morgan was a fan favorite. People fell in love with her story, her work ethic, and her refusal to give up. After the show was released, she had multiple people reaching out wanting to represent her. She signed with Creative Artists Agency and has gotten several endorsement deals, including one for Victoria's Secret Pink. Having cash in the bank has been such a weight off her shoulders. All the kids on the show who came from a place of insecurity—not knowing where their next meal was coming from—are now being given opportunities to work, meet fascinating people, and make actual money. People have asked if they're getting spoiled, but I haven't seen a second of that. They are all profoundly grateful.

These kids are like my own kids. My heart hurts when they hurt. And I have to get to know them to understand how to help them. I've always felt it was my job to learn how to reach these students while still making sure they knew I was on their side. If they were doing something wrong, I had to keep up their confidence while at the same time correcting their behavior.

Sometimes what a person needs can be so small. A former cheerleader named Marysa recently told me about a time in a preliminary round of nationals when she'd had a rough performance and was in her head about it. She said that when we were walking back to the bandshell where the final performance would be held I put my arm around her to talk her through what she'd done and to reassure her that we'd figure out how to fix it.

While we were talking, she'd picked up a lucky penny off the sidewalk and handed it to me. The next day as we went through warm-ups and headed to the on-deck area, I pulled Marysa aside and handed her back the penny. I told her to put it in her shoe.

Marysa nailed her performance. She said she thought it was because she had that little token of support: "That made me feel like you were right next to me every step of the routine and helped me slow my mind and focus on each section one at a time."

Very often all anybody needs is some small gesture of encouragement. My job, like that of any good manager, is to learn what motivates each member of my team, so my responsibilities in that regard change from day to day, whether I'm getting someone food that week because they don't have any money or letting them vent to me about something they're going through or giving them a pep talk that's going to lift them up when they feel the most down. This makes coaching a challenging job. And it means I need to be available to the team at all hours. The cheerleaders sometimes call me Mom and Chris Dad.

My phone has been known to ring in the middle of the night. Middle-of-the-night calls are never good news, are they? Someone's almost always in trouble. One fall night a few years ago, I was in a dead sleep and my phone rang. It was the campus police. They'd pulled over one of my girls and they thought she'd been drinking. The officer told me, "If you'll come up here and get her, we'll let her go."

Oh, I was so mad at her. But I wasn't going to let her sit there all night. I hustled: got dressed, drove up there, and took custody of her from the campus police. Their facility was on campus, right by the dorms. Still, I wasn't going to drive her to her front door and drop her off like an Uber driver.

I took her for a drive. She was sobbing and kept apologizing. I couldn't really tell if she was drunk, but it was the middle of the night, around 3 a.m. One thing I do know is that nothing good happens after midnight (when it comes to college students, the time cutoff may be even earlier), so it didn't really matter what the truth was. She had no business being out and about at that hour.

We drove by her building, and by a lot of other buildings, until we were on the other side of campus. I made her get out and walk home. I said, "I'll follow you, to make sure you're safe and no one snatches you, but I'm not taking you to your dorm. You need some time to think about what you did." And I trailed her the half mile or so as she walked home.

I believed that it wouldn't do her any good if I made it too easy on her. I was already sparing her a night in jail. I wasn't also going to chauffeur her to her front steps.

Her mom called me the next day and said, "My daughter told me you made her walk."

"I sure did," I said, no doubt sounding as sleepy as I felt after getting almost no sleep the night before. "I absolutely did. Did you have a problem with it?"

"Oh no!" her mother said. "No problem. Not at all."

"Okay then," I said. And I never got a call at three in the morning again—about that particular student.

Sometimes the kind of help my students need is financial. If a big group is going to go out to eat and I get word, "Well, this person is staying home because they don't have any money," then I know I need to step in and find them some way to make money. Often I have to get creative, because they have too much pride to ask for help. No one wants a handout. I get that and respect it. Sometimes I find work for them: some sort of clerical task or manual job. I've found students gigs teaching private tumbling lessons at the local gym. Often they just need that little boost to survive for a few more weeks until they get their student aid. Kids have pride, and in order to keep them motivated you can't take that away. It's my job as a coach to help them without making a big show about it.

Every summer, my team attends the three-day camp put on by the NCA at Southern Methodist University in Dallas. The camp typically hosts hundreds of cheerleaders and dancers from universities and colleges across many states. There's usually even a team from Mexico. Camp is where teams compete to earn a bid for the national championships.

Preparing for camp is our first experience together as a team, and the learning curve is steep as we jam a lot of work into a few short days. The kids are usually exhausted and sore by the time we leave for camp, so having some downtime to enjoy one another outside of the gym is well needed and deserved. To allow everyone to decompress and have some fun during that stressful time of preparation in the days before camp starts, I have the whole team over to my house for a pool party.

At the party, kids are everywhere: in the pool doing crazy flips off the diving board, eating and chatting on the porch, having an intense game of cornhole in the yard, stretching out on towels to catch some rays.

I also throw the team a party at Christmas. The Christmas party, one of my favorite times of the year, is another great time for us to come together and enjoy one another after a long semester of working hard. For most of my years coaching, I toiled over the stove cooking a big meal for the team. But I was always so exhausted from cooking. Finally, I got smart and started taking the team out for dinner at a restaurant. Then everyone comes back to my house for home-cooked desserts and gifts. We draw names in advance for Secret Santa gifts and have the most fun watching everybody open their gifts one at a time. The party lets us end the semester on a fun note before the kids go home for the holidays. Building that sense of community and those individual relationships is key to finding ways to work together so everyone does their absolute best. And it's my job to figure out what it takes to support them. What's going to motivate one person might not motivate another.

Everyone has different capacities. I'm not going to try to make a stunter do a complicated tumbling pass in the spotlight, and I'm not going to make a tiny flyer hold up two other girls. That's true for managing students in school, people in the workplace, and even for parenting. Your kids are going to be different from one another. I have to remember that even my own children respond to different forms of encouragement.

My daughter, Ally, is twenty and she's cheering now at Southern Methodist University near Dallas. She's been cheerleading basically since birth. As she grew up, I coached her in All Star cheer (a very popular club program among cheerleaders) until high school while she also did cheer at school. She's always been my easy kid, very independent and driven. She never needed me to push her to achieve. Her grades were excellent. She decided this summer that she wanted to go to law school after she graduates in May. She bought herself study guides for the LSAT and spent the entire summer studying. She recently received her scores. They were in the ninety-second percentile.

In high school, when Ally's boyfriend got a scholarship to play football at SMU, she decided to go to school there. I'm really happy she's there, because it's a prestigious school with excellent academics and it's only about fifty miles up the road from me. It's close enough for her to come home and visit or for us to drive up to see her. Chris and our son, Austin, go to all the football games there. I go to any that don't conflict with the Navarro football schedule.

Austin just turned twenty-four. He graduated from Texas Tech (which is six hours across the state) in 2017. He's smart, too, but unlike his sister, he's only ever done as much as he needed to get by. As he grew up, I had my thumb on him at all times with schoolwork and making sure he got things turned in. When he went away to Tech I wasn't going to just leave him to his own devices. I called him regularly to make sure he was up for class. I tend to do that a lot with my cheerleaders here, too—make sure that they're where they're supposed to be. I'm always stopping by their classrooms, looking to see if they're in there.

I've had a lot of experience with kids at this stage of life, just out on their own. They still often need a lot of guidance. Our culture seems to expect them to go from their parents' home to college and suddenly be automatically independent, but that's not realistic. When my son left the house, I had to keep after him to make sure he stayed on the right path. Young people don't want guidance, but most of them need it. Ultimately my son graduated in three years with a degree in public relations. When the show took off, he was right there with the know-how to help me deal with social media.

Even in terms of managing myself, I've realized that what I need as a coach has changed over time. Especially in the beginning, when I was in my early twenties, I tried not to get too close to the students. I wanted to make sure they knew that there was a separation, that I was not their friend even though we were the same age. I wanted them to have respect for me and to see me as their superior even if I was young and naïve and still learning.

Now that I'm older and closer to the age of their parents, I feel like I can let that guard down a little bit. I can see them obsessing over *Bad Girls Club* and think, *What is wrong with you that you love this show so much?* But I can also crack a smile and play along, let them pretend to throw a drink in my face, scream as if I'm pulling their hair.

This job requires that I take care of these kids to the absolute best of my ability. Figuring out who needs what—materially, emotionally, educationally—and how I can best help them is a huge responsibility and also a great honor. People come from all walks of life and each of us is built differently, but when you take the time to get to know how someone operates, you can learn how to be strategic in how to motivate them. The more secure I can make each student as an individual, the better we do as a team.

3

FIGHT TO GET ON MAT—
BUT BE GRACIOUS IF YOU'RE OFF

One of the toughest times for me every year is when I have to announce which twenty of our athletes will compete in the annual championship at Daytona—what we call being "on mat"—and who's not. I know that every single one of those kids wants to compete in the big event. Being competitive is part of being an athlete. They want to be on that outdoor stage in the Florida sun. And they came to the cheer program with that goal in mind. It's just that there will always be alternates. I can't get by with only twenty people on the team. If we have injuries or people who don't make their grades or who leave, we need backup, just like any team.

Everyone is talented, so there will be people who are not on mat even though they are certainly good enough to be on mat. They just didn't get chosen, for whatever reason. Putting together the right group to perform together is like assembling a puzzle. The right group has an unspoken understanding and a way of compensating for one another's weaker points and accentuating others' strengths. I'm looking to put all the pieces in the right place. Sometimes that means this person fits that spot, and sometimes it's this other person, based on something small and beyond their control.

Still, the kids who are off mat need to be completely engaged—they might need to step in at any moment, and we also need their emotional support. A bad attitude from just one team member can pull a lot of people down. So we have a conversation before we even pick mat: "Listen. This is what's going to happen. You're going to be spending a lot of time when you're not physically doing anything, and it's going to feel bad sometimes. You're going to feel like you're not important. But you *are*. And you'll begin to understand how important your role is when we start going full out."

Honestly, cheering from the sides—what we call mat talk—is the fuel that gets those twenty people through the routine, beginning to end. It's almost impossible to go full out in silence or with no one cheering for you. And that's why mat talk is so necessary. Not just from the people on the sides of the mat, but even from the members of the team performing. You have to encourage each other, even yell to feel that energy. Mat talk is one of the greatest gifts of cheerleading, and it's something each of us can use more of in all areas of our life.

When we were doing press for *Cheer* early in 2020, we were asked to film a segment for *The Late Show with Stephen Colbert*. To introduce it, Stephen began: "America has been gripped by the historic and deeply stressful event playing out on their televisions. Of course, I'm talking about the Netflix show *Cheer*."

He went on to identify the secret of the show's success—that people were inspired by how cheerleaders used "mat talk" to motivate one another. He said, "These stressful times, we could all use someone cheering us on like that, which is why tonight I'm proud to introduce *The Late Show*'s latest sponsor . . ."

It cut to an image of people looking sad and a voiceover: "Are you exhausted? Uninspired? Lacking the motivation to do even the simplest things? Then you need: Mat Talk for Regular People™, the only non-FDA approved, Netflix-based solution for small yet seemingly impossible tasks, like getting out of bed."

With that, two cheerleaders pop up from behind a woman's bed and start cheering for her. Then they and another cheerleader cheer for a man to go ahead and cross the street or a woman to speak up at work about the company's fourth-quarter numbers.

Then the ad described the "Coach Monica Booster Shot." I put my hand on the office woman's shoulder and said, "Listen. I picked you to send this email for a reason. You can do it." Then I walked a few feet away and whispered to someone, "I don't think she can do it."

The tagline: "Because you got tired from just <u>watching</u> *Cheer*." I love this skit because it really highlighted the one thing that the world seemed to obsess over—mat talk!

"Mat talk." Funny how this phrase that I've used for so long suddenly became a phenomenon after *Cheer* came out. As cheerleaders, our main job is to support our teams and rally up the fans when the game is on the line. It's already in our nature to cheer others on. So it's no surprise that cheering our own teammates on is one of the most natural things we can do, or that in our world being good at mat talk is one of the most cherished character traits.

Cheerleaders at the top of their field don't even have to be told to mat-talk one another. We can be at a practice and someone will be struggling with a skill. You will slowly notice a circle form around that person as the yelling of motivational talk gets louder and rowdier.

Why do we do this?

First of all, we have an innate sense of when someone is in need. We know that words are powerful and that the sound of those words—often being shouted with emotion—can send energy to someone who needs that extra push, extra adrenaline, and extra belief in themselves that they *can* do a skill, *can* hit a routine, *can* be successful.

Words are powerful.

What words do you say to yourself? Are they positive? Are you filling your mind with words of encouragement and self-love, or are you your own worst enemy, filling your mind with poison?

What words are you saying to your loved ones? Are you building up their self-esteem or are you tearing them down?

What words are you saying to your teammates and your coworkers? Are you encouraging them and trying to make everyone the best they can be so that your team is ready to excel? Or is jealousy getting in the way? Are you sacrificing the betterment of the team because of your own personal agenda?

We all have the ability to choose how we use words. We should choose wisely in all areas of our life. We are only as good as we *think* we can be. We are only as good as the people we surround ourselves with. We are only as good as our teammates. Let's build others up with mat talk—and let's start by mat-talking ourselves.

4

SEPARATE FANTASY
FROM REALITY

Mat talk is powerful because it's grounded in reality and draws our focus to the moment at hand. It's a good reminder to focus on what's right in front of you rather than spending all day dreaming of greener pastures.

My hometown, Corsicana, is a traditional, conservative small town in northeast central Texas. Growing up here, I thought, *Oh, I can't wait to get to the big city! I can't wait to get out of this little town!* I loved math, anything to do with numbers, and I went into finance for college. And I thought that Wall Street was the top of the top. You just couldn't get any better. If I could make it to Wall Street, I'd have made it. I had never been to New York, but the thought of being there seemed glamorous to me, and glamour seemed like something I would enjoy.

Now, the truth is, when I went to New York the first time, I was a little disappointed. Here's the thing: I like things to be orderly. I like everything tidy and clean. I admire Chris for his obsession with keeping our lawn perfectly manicured like it's a baseball diamond, not a blade of grass out of place. Downtown Corsicana is just as cute as can be. It is a historic place with lush greenery in front of the businesses and beautiful wide brick streets.

New York was really dirty! I was shocked at the trash set out in piles right in front of the buildings. And on that first trip to New York, which I'd heard described as the greatest city on earth, a giant rat walked right out in front of us on the sidewalk. It saw us coming and it *wasn't even scared*.

My first impression of New York was that it contained a lot of buildings, a lot of concrete, and a lot of trash. And I didn't go back to New York for quite some time. I had to face up to the ways in which my dreams for myself had been based on a lack of reality. Why was Wall Street my goal? Why did I think that was the only way to achieve success?

As it turned out, because I stayed in Corsicana, my luck found me. Not only have I been able to reach the top of my profession, but the cost of living is low, my commute to work is a relaxing fifteen minutes, and there's no traffic! I always said I wanted to live in a big city. But now when I drive to Dallas, I think, *How do people do this every day?*

Many of my students have come back to Navarro to tell me that the four-year colleges they were so eager to get in to wound up being less thrilling than the idealistic brochures suggested. Again and again, I see the young people I coach find their ideas about themselves upended. They had one idea of who they were and what they wanted. Then reality showed up and they found, usually, that they were capable of even more.

One huge myth I've seen debunked in a lot of people's minds over the past few years is the idea of what a cheerleader is. The cheerleader stereotype, which you see in nearly every cheerleading movie, is that we're all rich, popular, mean girls who are always fighting with one another. And that's not true of cheerleading at all. I think *Cheer* has done a lot to separate the fantasy of the cheerleader from the reality. When the show came out, I got so many messages that said, "I had no idea that y'all did things like that. I had no idea that cheerleaders worked that hard. I had no idea that cheerleaders weren't all rich and popular!"

I will qualify that: it's possible that it *was* somewhat true back when the only kind of cheerleading was school-based and cheerleaders were chosen by vote. If everyone has to try out in front of peers, it could be the case that the girls who are picked are just the most well-liked. And if your coach is really just a science or English teacher who coaches on the side, your routines probably won't be all that ambitious.

But that is not at all what cheerleading is today. In the late 1980s, independent All Star cheer gyms started to show up around the country, and throughout the 1990s the sport exploded. These gyms were outside of the school's social structure. What was rewarded was talent, hard work, and devotion—*not* popularity.

Some kids start training in All Star at three years old and they're coached by former cheerleaders who really know what they're doing.

As a coach, I've seen the general talent level rise over the years. Unlike in the early days, when I might have most kids trying out with no experience at all, now I'm getting kids who have been training hard for fifteen years.

When I was a little girl, there wasn't yet All Star cheerleading. All we had was a gymnastics program in a front yard down the street from me. When I was very little, I would walk over. The coaches had mats out in the grass, and a little set of bars and a beam. I would just sit on the curb and watch, longing to take part. For years, I begged my parents, "Please let me do this. I want to do gymnastics so badly!"

It took a long time, but finally they said okay. I was in fifth grade by that point (which is ancient to start gymnastics or cheer by today's standards!). Knowing I had to play catch-up, I gave it everything I had. I learned bars, beam, vault, and floor work. Soon after, I was able to start school cheer. I only got to compete once a year, whereas kids today in All Star are going to competitions all the time, building up to nationwide and even worldwide competitions.

I was finishing up high school when I first heard about All Star. If I'd only had that opportunity as a young girl, I would have thrived. But I'm grateful that I've been able to experience it vicariously through my daughter.

As is routinely pointed out in online cheer forums, All Star is expensive. It can cost families thousands of dollars a year between gym fees, uniforms, and travel to competitions. But the payoff is so great that you see families make sacrifices. Parents might work two or three jobs to keep kids in the program. If you're in All Star, you tend to stay out of trouble: you're in the gym all the time, and you're focused. It gives you a purpose. Even parents without a lot of extra income fight hard to give their kids this opportunity. A lot of these kids find All Star gyms to be their happy place, somewhere they can go and find themselves, make good friends, and develop new skills every day.

Another thing All Star did for the sport was encourage more boys to become cheerleaders. As a rule, fewer boys than girls want to participate in cheerleading, so boys are often able to get scholarships or discounts. Early on, a lot of the boys who cheered in Navarro had played football in high school. They knew how to do stunts because they had girlfriends who did gymnastics or cheer and would say, "Hey, you're strong! Throw me into this stunt!"

Cheer was such an eye-opener for people who had only seen the mean-girl cheerleading movies. I cherish the shocked messages I've gotten from viewers: "These aren't the kind of people that we thought cheered! We had no idea they came from all different types of backgrounds, had no idea that they were athletic, had no idea that they had grit and determination and resiliency like other top-notch athletes!"

I'm so glad the world is finally seeing what I know: that cheerleaders are as tough as any other athletes—and often, in my opinion, even tougher. We're not the mean girls of the movies. But I understand how tough it can be to let go of early ideas. We need to stay open and flexible to let ourselves learn the truth about things.

Thanks to the show, I was able to go back to New York City after that first trip. This time around, I discovered the city's strengths: Broadway, restaurants, diversity. I was able to see its beauty in a way I wasn't when I was distracted by the rats and trash. With members of my family and my cheer team, I walked down crowded sidewalks full of energy, ate delicious food, and even saw the real Wall Street— not as it was in my fantasy when I was in my twenties but as a stop on my sightseeing tour as a winning coach surrounded by loved ones. Sometimes reality and fantasy meet in the loveliest ways.

5

BE ACCOUNTABLE
TO YOUR TEAM

Have you ever been on a team or worked with a person who always has what you could only call negative energy? The kind of person who talked trash all the time, was bitter about others' success, and around whom there was always some kind of drama? I've had the displeasure of coaching people and working with people who fit into this category. And in both cases, I found it to be exhausting.

One year I had a girl on my team who was the epitome of "woe is me." From the very beginning of the semester I was dealing with conflicts she had with one teammate after another. She kept provoking people and then being baffled as to why she was always involved in conflict. And she invented lavish theories about why no one wanted to stunt with her or hang out with her after practice.

One day during a break from practice she came to talk to me and started crying. She said so-and-so didn't like her and everyone was out to get her and wah, wah, wah. Usually when my cheerleaders cry I am profoundly moved, but in her case, I knew too much of the backstory.

"I don't have any friends!" she told me. "Everywhere I go, it's the same thing!"

I had to deliver a hard truth.

"Okay, let's look at the common factor here," I said. "Everywhere *you* go, there's drama. What do you think the common factor is? It looks like it's you. Could it be that you're the one creating all this drama? Based on what you're saying, I think that you're creating this environment for yourself. And if you're looking for trouble, that's exactly what you're going to find."

I tried to help her see that all these people she thought were out to get her were busy with their own lives. They were not thinking about her nearly as much as she thought they were. They were not plotting against her. They were not going out of their way to not be her friend. If they didn't particularly want to be around her, frankly, I didn't blame them. She complained all day, every day. She was always seeing the worst in everyone and every situation. She never found joy in any aspect of life. She didn't show others the consideration and care that she demanded from them. I wasn't surprised that she only lasted one year in the program.

Her life didn't change in that moment I spoke with her but I hope that she at least stopped for a second to look in the mirror and ask herself, "Is it possible that I am playing a role in how my own life is going?"

The biggest problem wasn't even that she was a downer. It was that she never looked within to question her own motivations and actions.

This is a question I insist everyone on the team ask: What part am *I* playing in any problems here?

We all make mistakes, no matter how hard we may try not to. What we *do* about our errors is the important thing. Owning up and taking responsibility for them is key to being a good team member and a good leader. So many people just want to be right all the time. And if they're not right, they want to pretend that it doesn't matter. They don't want to take accountability for their shortcomings. That's why we can't meet in the middle on so many issues. Nobody wants to say, "Wait a minute. Maybe I got this wrong." If we all practiced self-accountability, the world would be a much better place.

I do everything I can to model the behavior I'm trying to teach. I show up every single day prepared. I don't make excuses when life gets tough. I self-reflect and analyze how I could have done a better job. I own up to bad decisions and apologize when needed. I try to never let people down.

And I try to call my team's attention to instances of others' accountability so they don't take it for granted, and I remind them of the ways we all rely on one another. If someone tries to tell me that it doesn't matter if she doesn't go to class, I point out that the teacher is there to teach her. If the student isn't there it can mess things up for the teacher, who's now going to have to repeat himself; for her lab partner, who will have to do all the work that day; for the friend she's now going to ask for class notes. I try to turn things around: "What if you had studied hard for a test and your teacher didn't show up to administer it? How is that going to affect you? What if your friend was always sleeping in and then asking for your notes? How would you feel about her?"

I try to teach my cheerleaders by example that there is strength in admitting you were wrong, whether that's in a relationship or in your work or in saying something that was out of place or out of line. On the team it could be something as simple as taking owner-ship of the fact that you were late. Taking ownership of the fact that you didn't show up for someone when they needed you.

When you take ownership after making an error, I'm going to respect you ten times more than if you got defensive and made excuses. That's a huge step for us all in terms of being able to work together instead of fighting or working against one another. This is critical in your relationships, too. If you're not taking accountabil-ity for your actions, that's how you get divorced—and I know this because I've been there, done that!

This is such an important issue for me that I've instituted a gym policy that forces the kids to see how their actions affect others: I punish the whole squad if one of their members does something wrong.

Specifically, if any one of them is late, they are required to do five back tucks (backward flips in a tucked position—they're exhausting) for each offense. For more serious infractions I make them all run laps. (They hate that.) Everyone has to bring their running shoes to practice in case they have to run to atone for something any one of them has screwed up, whether that's breaking rules or skipping class.

I tell them all on the first day: "Your actions affect others. So when you don't go to class, the whole team is going to run. I'm hoping that you feel bad about that. That's the whole purpose, for it to motivate you enough not to want others to be disciplined because of your poor decision."

The other great effect of this form of discipline is that the whole team begins to work on getting the best out of one another. Roommates make sure everyone's up. They text each other if they're not in class a couple of minutes before it starts—"Where are you? Get to class! I don't want to run!"

Some of this is self-interest, even on my part. I want them to understand that what they do affects everyone, including me. If one of my cheerleaders does something wrong, I'm going to get a call from my athletic director. I'll have to explain what went wrong, and if it's something really bad, my job could be on the line. That's real life. People at the top are held accountable for the people that work for them. If someone puts something dumb out on social media, then suddenly upper management needs to take action.

Self-accountability can prove particularly transformative for those students who come from rough home situations—and that's many of the kids at Navarro. They can choose to either use that tragedy to give them strength or to feel sorry for themselves and use it as a cop-out. I am so disappointed when a student who's bursting with talent and energy says, "Well, I got the short end of the stick. That means I didn't have the same opportunity as everyone else and so of course I won't go as far."

What I try to make them see is that the gym is a place where no matter where you come from you have the same opportunity as everyone else. And if you've had to struggle, you're even more likely to succeed, because you're tough. You create your own path. If you're making excuses, you're just going to stay where you are. You need to use any hardships to motivate yourself to move forward.

The students I see pushing themselves the hardest are the ones who take full accountability for their futures. They say, "I don't want to live like I came up. I want to do more than my parents did and more than anyone expected of me."

One former student of mine grew up in the foster care system. His own parents were never around and he was sexually abused as a kid. He did not have structure, love, or role models to teach and nurture him. But he knew he wanted more in his life, and he knew that he wanted to create a family that was far different from the way he grew up. And he did exactly that. He went to college. He steered clear of drugs. He married his college sweetheart and has a wonderful job and two beautiful children. His children are secure and cared for, and they know they're loved. He's broken the cycle of abuse that he was born into, and I could not be prouder of him.

Whatever your ambition, you need to go and fight hard for it, and be the best employee, the best teammate, the best partner in a relationship. You can be all these things, but you have to take ownership when you struggle. No one is perfect. We're all going to make mistakes. As you're navigating through your relationships or work, take ownership when you've done wrong, and make it right and try to do better.

It takes a while for young kids to truly understand this. Every chance I get, I tell them to flip the situation, to develop empathy. Not that they always immediately shape up, but at least it's an opportunity to think about it! And little by little, they grow.

I see this sort of dilemma play out in my students' lives all the time. A student will say, "Oh, somebody's having a party. I really want to go to that, so I'm just going to call in sick to work."

I want them to stop the second they get that invite and think: *But how would that affect other people?*

If you call in sick when you're really not, now your boss has to call someone else to see if they can come in to take your spot. Maybe it's that person's day off but she's a good employee, so even though she had plans of her own, now she's going to show up. So because you wanted to go to a party you've messed up this coworker's day. Or maybe your boss can't find someone to take up the slack, and now everybody that night is running around working twice as hard. None of us lives in a bubble. All of life is collaborative.

I see this in parenting as well. Selfish parents don't take responsibility for the effect they have on their children's well-being. If you decide that you still want to go out every night, drinking with your friends rather than staying home to be there for your kids, who's suffering? Your children. They don't get the benefit of you being present in their life, or experiencing a good role model, or having someone show up to their games. It's something I've seen in my students' home lives and it breaks my heart every time.

Young people usually need to hear an idea repeated many times before they can fully understand it. Some get it right away, but often you'll have to drill it into them over a year or more before they have the epiphany. Still, having the whole team run for one cheerleader's mistake has proved especially effective.

As I watch the kids run around and around, I notice that the person who caused it looks hugely guilty that they've put the team in this situation. Often before the second lap they will come over and say, "Please. I will run ten times more if you just don't make anybody else run!"

That's exactly what I want to hear.

I always say no.

In my experience, the lesson is only driven home if the person sees her friends sweaty and exhausted on that track because she decided to sleep in that morning. You better believe from then on she'll be setting multiple alarms and never skipping class again.

Being accountable to your team—whether that team is your squad, your family, or your company—can help keep you grounded. Sure, there is added responsibility if your actions might let someone else down, but being part of something bigger than yourself offers up just as many additional rewards. When you show up for others, they'll show up for you, too.

6

LEAD BY EXAMPLE

The new president of Navarro College, Dr. Kevin G. Fegan, is incredibly charismatic. I find him so inspiring that I'll leave meetings raring to work longer hours. That's how I want to feel about all leaders.

That's true of Navarro's new athletic director, Michael Landers, too. For years, Landers was a successful basketball coach. Now, as my boss, he's shown himself to be an incredible leader. He's organized, he's got great ideas, and he's very engaged at all times. I loved our last director, but Landers has reinvented the position. He recently started the Navarro College Hall of Fame (which I was inducted into last year with nine other Bulldogs past and present—a big thrill for us all). He holds meetings almost every week. One of his real gifts is his ability to communicate to us why something is important or what it is he needs from each team. He's always reaching out to the coaches in the department with questions like, "Hey, what community service have you done lately?" Every day, he's checking in and making sure we're on our toes. It motivates us all to work smarter.

Humility has made me a better coach and a better leader. Leadership starts with you. You can't try to change other people if you're not working on yourself. Yes, I'm on top. I'm the coach. But we're all in this together. When it comes to getting the job done, I don't have an ego. I don't mind picking up trash off the ground. I'm not going to yell at someone else to do it when it is right in front of me. I'll go and get the plunger and unclog the toilet if I need to, because everyone needs to see that if there's a problem, somebody has got to fix it.

If you lead that way, if you're the one who's willing to sacrifice, others will pick up on that behavior. They're not going to leave at night until they know that every little tape roll is picked up and thrown away. And those are the people I admire the most. Nobody is too good for a job, and leadership should never be used to stroke your ego. True leaders bring people together to work as a team, to do the best job that they can for whatever goal they're working for. The team *and* the leader help each other get there. If you are going to build a championship culture in any atmosphere, you want to lead by example.

On the first day of every season I give the squad a big talk about this. Because it doesn't matter what you say. It matters what you do. You'll see some second- or third-year team members feel powerful because they're team veterans. They can become almost drunk with power.

I tell them: "You think you're powerful because you've done this before. But you don't have any power unless you are leading by example. You shouldn't even have to open your mouth. People are watching you, and they're going to either want to be like you or they're not. If you want to say, 'Hey, so-and-so, you should do XYZ!' then make sure you've done X and Y and Z to the best of your ability and with a good attitude. If they have respect for you because you work the hardest—you're there early, you're there afterward picking up trash, you're going above and beyond—they're going to listen to every word you say. And that's not because you're a veteran, but because they respect and admire you."

I've had many veteran cheerleaders who were extremely talented but who lacked leadership qualities. I always find that disappointing. When someone has incredible skills, I develop high expectations and then I'm surprised when they don't fulfill them. This sometimes leads to awkward conversations in which they talk about how they are the best members of the team because of their skills and I have to explain that there's more to it than that. You can have the best skills I've ever seen, but if you're not someone I can trust and someone who motivates those around you, you don't strengthen my team. If all you have is a good skill set, that's not going to impress me as much as good skills combined with all the other wonderful qualities that make a good leader: integrity, confidence, empathy, self-accountability, resilience, humility, good communication, and the ability to inspire others.

Then you have those kids who stand out. I've had many kids come through my program who have inspired me. Specifically, one year I had a male cheerleader who had that special quality—a presence about him that people were drawn to. He was soft-spoken, yet people listened when he talked. It was hard to put your finger on just what it was that made his words so engaging and comforting, and yet everything he said seemed to make people feel better. He was a role model both on the mat and in the classroom. He had a deep passion for the sport of cheerleading and his work ethic was unparalleled, but he also had the ability to show compassion and bring people together for a common goal. He was a true leader and I was blessed to be his coach.

I tell my team: "Do you want to be that person who's all talk? Because I really don't care what comes out of your mouth. It could be some great, inspiring words, but nobody will listen to them if you talk about one thing and do something else."

If we're having to do back tucks because you were late, or if we have to run for you because you didn't go to class, or you aren't really pushing yourself the hardest—well, then it doesn't matter what kind of things you want to say as a leader. They won't want to hear it from you, and neither will I.

One way I try to model behavior is to speak with the same calm self-control I want everyone to exhibit. In the gym, I show the kids the same respect that I would want shown to me. When I have a problem with someone I usually pull them to the side and have a conversation about the problem at hand. I do not like to embarrass anyone, which is why most of my conversations are private. I give each student an opportunity to express their feelings but also try to make sure they see both sides of the situation.

I am not here to manage people by yelling at them and threatening them. Instead, I am here to lead and inspire them to become more and do more than they ever imagined. It is very rare that I lose my temper, and the kids know that if I ever do it must be because something has gone very, very wrong. When two kids start arguing with each other and won't let me break it up rationally, maybe then I have to be the crazy person. Then they are so shocked they can't even remember why they were fighting with each other.

7

A $5 PLANNER CAN
CHANGE EVERYTHING

Every year since I began teaching decades ago I've seen fresh-men arrive at college without knowing even the basics of managing their time. This year there's the added stress of COVID-19, but otherwise the first week of the semester has arrived the same way it arrives every year: in total chaos.

I always start each semester the same way: months in advance, I send out an email to each of the students explaining what they need to do to prepare for the term. It's a lot of information, but I try to simplify it as much as possible. While I would prefer to write these notes as inspiring and enthusiastic letters, I have learned to take my fellow teachers' advice and to present the information in clear, bullet-pointed lists rather than as full sentences.

Now, were I a student receiving such an important message, *I* would print out this email and use a highlighter and get right to work, but I understand that many young people today don't arrive at college with that tendency. My generation took notes by hand. If you objected to a grade, you had to physically go talk to a teacher. If I sat down to do homework, there wasn't a phone to play on or social media or anything like that to distract me. Young adults today have grown up with cell phones and with parents who might not have taught them quite as much independence. Still, it's frustrating.

In this year's bullet-pointed email, sent early in the summer, I explained to the newcomers what they had to do, from sending in their official high school transcripts to applying for housing.

It's a lot of stuff to do, but none of it is terribly difficult. And yet, many of the students don't take care of these things right away and then they forget. And then it's August.

I have a group chat set up for the cheer team, and I send reminders to the group: "Hey guys, this is what needs to be done!" I even say, "Forward the email to your parents if they're the ones helping you."

Most years, when we all meet up at cheer camp in July I take care of any stragglers and make sure they get everything done. But this year camp was canceled because of COVID, so dorm move-in week arrived in mid-August and a bunch of students were still missing one or more of their required documents.

We did a Zoom call and I said, "Guys, some of y'all still haven't even applied for housing. You have to do these things!"

Then, as a follow-up, my assistant Kailee and I sat and texted each student individually, telling them, "This is what you need."

Still, so many things were missing. In one week of constant harassment I got the group from twenty-five needing to register to five needing to register. But still, five is a lot!

Finally, move-in week arrived. I wrote everyone and said: "This is the end of me bugging you. Now don't come find me if you're not allowed to check into housing because you haven't taken the TSI or something!" Then they know it's serious and suddenly everyone's taking the TSI test—that's the Texas Success Initiative assessment test that determines whether a student is ready for college-level work in certain subjects—that very afternoon.

A huge part of my job as a coach is to make it extremely clear to everyone who cheers for me that school comes first. Athletics are important, but what's more important is leaving college with a degree and being prepared for life outside of the cheer team.

To that end, I encourage everyone to buy a planner the first week of the school year so they can keep track of every assignment and every practice. You can look ahead to the coming weeks or months of tests and plan out your studying in the time you have leading up to them. You can keep track of friends' birthdays, doctor's appointments, and bill payments. You can circle our competitions and see how many more practices you have to get the routine down.

Yes, it's mundane. But keeping track of everything and being organized is the foundation for other good habits: showing up on time, remembering other people's special days. Living by the planner means you're accountable to others. You can be relied upon. You are always where you say you'll be. These are the kinds of people I want on my team and that people like having as friends and as employees.

I practice what I preach. I keep a planner, too, and I write every day in my spiral notebook. It's full of plans for the team, notes about who should be on mat, and ideas for everything from uniforms to formations.

Seeing it in black and white like that helps you keep track of your obligations and of how much you have to do each week. The planner is about more than showing up for appointments. Keeping track of your schedule and planning ahead can help you carve out study time for exams, figure out how much time you have to complete assignments, and pencil in things to look forward to once you've finished your work.

Some team members push back, telling me that they only want to cheer and not think about school, but they quickly learn that on my team, living by the planner and working hard in school are non-negotiable.

I hear from former students all the time that they understand now why I put that much emphasis on school. One male cheerleader who now has a master's degree and works as an assistant principal recently wrote me a note that melted my heart. He said he'd arrived at Navarro in 1999 as "a hot mess." He had no plans other than to cheer for two years. He said I'd asked him about his classes every single day and made it clear that school came first. He realized that if he wanted to do what he'd come to do—cheer—he'd have to keep his grades up. That was the incentive he needed to make school a priority, and thus to stay on top of his planner.

He also told me something I hadn't known before: that his parents hadn't been present and that some in his family hadn't stood by him when he came out as gay. Cheerleading gave him an inner as well as an outer strength. Today, he's in a doctoral program, working with English-language learners. He wrote me: "Thanks to you, here I am twenty years later, still knowing the importance of school first."

Another devotee of the planner, a former cheerleader named Michael, told me that he still hears my voice in his head many years later telling him, "If you leave this program a better person, I did my job correctly!" He'd always struggled in school and had seen it as a chore he had to complete in order to qualify for his true love, cheer.

But being on our team and getting that planner changed him. He said, "As you start to practice day in and day out, subconsciously that mindset starts to take root in other aspects of your life—your friendships, relationships, and, most importantly for me, my academic life." Michael finished his first semester at Navarro with a 3.42 GPA. His high school GPA had been 1.42.

The $5 planner is a real tool, but it's also a metaphor: What cheap, easily available resource do you have access to that could be a game-changer? There's the outdoors for exercise (walking or jogging or biking); the right friend to encourage you to meet your goals; community groups within which you can develop a shared interest; not to mention the library (so old school!) for finding out more about something you want to pursue.

Another answer for a lot of young people that I know is junior college. As college costs soar, many people around the country, especially outside of major cities, are finding that they can't afford to attend prestigious four-year universities right out of high school. And so they go to a two-year college like Navarro. That way, they get an associate degree very cheaply and knock out all of their basic requirements. When they're done, they usually have a better sense of what they want to focus on and better work habits. They can either go into the workforce at that point or transfer to a four-year school as a junior in a major they are fairly certain about.

Obviously, I'm a little biased because I work at a community college, but I don't know why every student doesn't consider this, even if they have the cash on hand to go somewhere fancier. I think that the value of a junior or community college is something a lot of people don't realize. Often people who go off to a four-year university want the elite campus experience, like the big game day with the nationally recognized football team. If that's your goal—if it's worth potentially many thousands of dollars more to you to get to wear the shirt of some well-known college—then go for it.

But when you're looking at most people in America, your middle-class families and lower, it makes no sense at all to go straight to an expensive four-year school. At junior college, not only can you take those general requirement classes for much less money than you'll pay at a university, you'll also probably have smaller classes and more help from teachers. In addition, it's a great way to transition more gradually from high school to a university.

Some kids are naturally mature and independent from an early age, but many need time to grow socially, academically, and emotionally. They need time to make mistakes on a small scale without huge consequences so they can learn to be responsible adults at their own pace.

Too often we expect kids who have spent their high school lives surrounded by parents and siblings and having all their needs met to suddenly know how to be out there on their own: how to stick to a grocery budget, keep from getting lonely, track all the quizzes and tests and projects they're assigned. Given how steep the learning curve is, being on your own for the first time can be easier somewhere in your home state and with kids close to your age, without the pressure of a name school and all that it entails.

We tend to look at things that are expensive as being more special or more useful. But things we have close by—a community college, a paper planner—can change our lives far more than things that cost exponentially more. My team's victories over the years have proven this message to me again and again. We're a tiny little school in an overlooked part of the world, but when we show up to compete, we come to win.

8

SUPPORT YOUR COMMUNITY. IF YOU CAN'T, FIND ANOTHER COMMUNITY

One of the highlights of my life is Navarro College volleyball. We got a new volleyball coach last year and his first year on the job, the team went undefeated. The volleyball season is close to thirty games, and they didn't lose one. The final game in the national tournament was held in Kansas. The cheer team took an eight-hour bus ride so that we could sit in the stands and cheer on Navarro's players that night.

We'd become so invested in that coach and his incredible players that we were beside ourselves with excitement. During that last match in Kansas, I was sweating and biting my nails. We were riveted. We weren't showing off our elite stunting and tumbling skills or anything, but we had our megaphones and we were mat-talking them within an inch of their lives as the lead went back and forth. Finally it got down to the last round and . . .

They did it! We started jumping and screaming like we'd won ourselves. We gave the team a few moments to celebrate on their own before we ran onto the floor to get in on the group hug. We joined the victory circle—high-fiving everyone and telling them how amazing it all was, just beside ourselves with joy.

It was the best game I've ever been to.

After the tournament, some of the organizers mentioned how obsessed the Navarro cheerleaders were. I even had another cheer coach that was there DM'ing me and tell me how impressed he was. And we weren't doing anything involving elite skills. We were simply pouring our hearts out and giving the volleyball girls every bit of energy we had. That's real community—a true, shared goal.

Sometimes it's harder to be completely invested.

I love football. I'm a die-hard fan. My team has always been the Dallas Cowboys, bless them. Lord, it's been a long time since we were successful, but we're still hanging in there. When Chris and I were in college and went back to Corsicana to visit family, we would make sure we left in time to get back to Austin before ESPN *SportsCenter* came on, so we could see what everybody's stats were and how Troy Aikman, Emmitt Smith, and Michael Irvin did. Those were the days!

It can be awfully hard to cheer full out for a whole football game. Those games are long! If it's 105 degrees and we're standing outside with no shade for hours on end on the sidelines, or if it's raining or freezing and you're winning by sixty points, it's tough to sustain that level of enthusiasm for several hours. But we do it. We can't help ourselves.

The hottest game I can remember was a couple of years ago. The fall had been unnaturally hot. On this particular afternoon I tried to keep everyone's energy high even though we were all bright red and covered in sweat. When our team scored I tried to jump and cheer but my feet felt strange. I thought I'd stepped in gum. Then I looked down and realized the soles of my boots had melted off. The track that we were on was that hot. As I made my way to the fence, my soles kept flopping around. I had to get athletic tape and wrap my soles back onto my boots so I could walk. We still cheered the whole game. That's our job: we support our teams.

I've always felt that way about all the communities I'm in: my school, my church, my state, my country. But a few years back I was attending a church that made me feel uncomfortable at times. I began to question whether or not I was at the right place for me and my family. I wasn't sure if I could continue to keep cheering on those particular sidelines.

One Sunday at church our pastor gave a sermon in which he spoke on the topic of gay marriage. He said he would never marry two gay people. I'd always respected how traditional the pastor was, but the way he was talking that day did not feel traditional— it felt cruel. What he said went directly against my belief that all people should have equal rights and be treated the same. There were plenty of gay people who attended this church. I kept thinking, *How must they feel to be told by someone who's supposed to live in the spirit of God that they're not as good or worthy as the person next to them?*

Stuff like that eats at me. For anyone to feel as though they're less than another person because of who they're in love with, or the person that they want to be with?

I listen to the bestselling Christian author Jen Hatmaker's podcast. For Pride Month 2020, she had her daughter on as a guest. Her daughter, who is gay, grew up in a very spiritual family and attended every camp, youth group, and Bible study group. She movingly described the feeling of not being affirmed by the church. She said that people would say to her, "We love you anyway." She said she didn't want to be loved *anyway*, she wanted to be loved for the sum total of who she was, even the parts that some members of her church didn't yet fully understand.

Stories like that have convinced me over the years that it's not enough to tolerate difference—we must *actively* love one another and make it clear that *all* are welcome. And so on that particular Sunday when my pastor preached about gay marriage, I posted something about the sermon on Facebook and made it clear just how much I disagreed with it. I didn't name the pastor, but of course he knew who he was. When he saw the post, he called me and we had a long conversation on the phone. I made sure to say everything I felt about it. I asked him, "How would you feel if it was your child who was gay and wanted to get married? What if it were *you*?"

This was how I felt hearing him say those words about gay people: these are my *kids* he was talking about. How do you look at one of these magnificent young people—hardworking, honest, brave—and tell them they don't deserve the same kind of love or partnership or legal rights that other people have? Or tell them that you still love them *anyway.* "Anyway." As if it were a defect in their character not to be heterosexual. I've seen all too clearly how much damage that one little word can do to a young person. I wept on the phone as I tried to explain this to the pastor.

I believe in the Bible, certainly, but when it comes to perfectly following every letter, don't we all to one extent or another live in glass houses? There are many verses that directly state that fornicators and adulterers are not inheriting the Kingdom of God. Also, the Bible clearly states that a man and woman should not divorce, and if they do and remarry, then they are committing adultery. This pastor had certainly performed marriage ceremonies for plenty of people with these supposed shortcomings. Now, I don't understand how you pick and choose what you want to stick to so sternly out of the Bible. Better, I think, to go by the spirit of love and compassion.

Anyway, the pastor and I had a very open conversation. He seemed emotional, too. And at the end of this conversation, I said, "You know what? We're just going to have to agree to disagree, and I'll see you at church Sunday."

At that point, Chris and I both started to ask ourselves if we were at the right church for us. (Chris may have been even more angry about the sermon than I was.) As much as I loved other things about this pastor, I realized we'd need to start looking at other places.

The deciding factor was that I knew I shouldn't feel as if I couldn't invite my cheerleaders to attend services with me. I've had gay cheerleaders say, "I really want to reconnect with religion. Where can I go to church?" I realized that given the pastor's beliefs, I didn't feel safe inviting them to my church. That was a problem.

So about a year and a half ago Chris and I started going to another church. It's also technically a Baptist church, but it's called Grace Community and it really lives up to its name. This is a place where everyone is made to feel welcome and where everyone is shown grace. And when I bring my cheerleaders with me I know they will only hear what they should be hearing: that God loves them—period, no exceptions, no "anyway."

My faith is so important to me. It has gotten me through the toughest times in my life. I rely on prayer. Most of my prayers are a short conversation with God, simply thanking Him for the blessings in my life. When I am going through hard times, I ask Him for guidance and strength to make it through whatever the challenge is.

At the end of each cheer practice, a team member says a prayer and we end with the team repeating the Serenity Prayer: "God grant me the serenity to accept the things I cannot change, the courage to change the things I can, and the wisdom to know the difference."

I make it clear that you don't have to be Christian to share this wish for calmness and for hope, and that faith comes in many forms. What I wish for each of my team members, no matter their beliefs or who they are, is that they feel safe and loved, and that they know they can always come to me for protection and support. I believe that whoever they are they're all God's children—and my kids, too.

9

TALK AND TALK
AND TALK SOME MORE

The first time Chris and I got married, it was January of 1994. I was twenty-one and had just graduated college a semester early, in December of '93. We had a very traditional wedding in our church and then a reception at the country club, where there was an open bar—probably not the best idea.

We had a live band that our good friend Jason Manning played in. The alcohol was flowing, the dance floor was popping, and great memories were being made. The stories I later heard about after-parties included hook-ups, break-ups, and even one of my bridesmaids throwing up in my bed. But the craziness began before Chris and I even left the reception. Some of the guys insisted on shoe-polishing the limo. When the driver objected, there was a small altercation that got a little physical. The limo driver was red-faced and fuming by the time Chris and I got to the end of the line that had formed to bid us farewell. His glasses were broken and hanging sideways as he opened the door for us.

Then of course we spent the rest of the night being chauffeured by the world's angriest limo driver.

We can laugh about it now as a wild time, but a few years into our marriage it felt like maybe that scuffle had been a bad omen.

The trouble started when Chris and I became parents. It shocked our system. You go from being completely independent to suddenly having so much responsibility. In one day, my whole world changed. Suddenly, I couldn't even go to the grocery store without packing up this other little person and all that gear. And I felt like so much of the hard stuff fell to me as the mother. I heard myself speaking to Chris, a man I'd loved since our teen years, with dripping sarcasm: "Oh, you're going to go hunting this weekend? Well, I hope you *have fun.*"

Marriage is tough, and having kids while you're trying to manage your relationship and your job is even tougher—a whole new dimension of responsibility. Anybody who has children knows that. Now you're solely responsible for the care of these children—not just physically but mentally. It's a very important role, constantly battling to make the right decisions. *Am I spending enough time with my kids? Am I being a good enough example?* When you have a full-time job on top of that, you have serious stress.

Learning how to live with less independence took some time to figure out. Having babies can be one of the hardest times of your life. You don't sleep. You worry. I was working a lot while we were trying to raise these young children. And our marriage suffered. It can be easy to forget to take care of each other. In 2006, things reached a crisis point: we got a divorce.

We tried really hard to put the kids' feelings first and to make sure they wouldn't be too traumatized. We tried our best to coparent and not let issues we had with each other affect the kids. Austin was nine and Ally was six. They seemed to be handling it all well, but I knew it was still very hard on them. I felt terrible guilt. My dream when I got married and had children was to keep my family together forever. I always promised myself that if we hit a rough patch I would fight for my marriage. Both Chris and I are very family-oriented. We were high school sweethearts. It's not like each of us wasn't the love of the other's life. And yet the stress got to us.

I was resentful when he went on trips with his friends and I stayed back with the kids. He told me that I could do the same, go somewhere with my friends. You would think that would pacify me, but it did not. I didn't go anywhere. I stayed frustrated, and I took it out on him.

I found myself starting to keep score, and Chris did the same. We were both taking mental notes: who unloaded the dishwasher, who folded the clothes, who spent more money, and so on. I'm sure it will come as no surprise to you that each of us would have sworn up and down that we had a far superior score. Score-keeping is never a healthy activity in a marriage, yet there we were, and with every tally we grew further apart.

It also didn't help that I always had to be right and never apologized. To make things worse, I would just get angry and silent. Red flag! No communication! It was like we had a hole in our ship and we were slowly sinking. We became convinced that if we didn't jump off we would drown.

My own parents had divorced when I was twenty-two, and it was not pretty. I did not want my children ever to have to face the dilemmas I had: "Okay, we're going to spend Christmas over here with my mother, and then we're going to do Christmas with my father that night. . . ."

When Chris and I split, it was a hard time on all four of us. I saw my own children struggling to manage their time between two households and packing their bags every other weekend. And I felt like I'd failed.

And yet, divorce made us take the time to reflect on ourselves. I realized that I had to learn how to apologize. I had been very stubborn before. Not that I'm not stubborn now! But I began to admit that I'm not always right all the time. I *think* I'm always right, but deep down, I know I'm not. After a year apart, Chris and I both admitted we'd made mistakes and wanted to be married again, just without all the animosity.

We started dating each other for the first time since we were teenagers, and we got to experience the joy of falling in love all over again. I had read so many books about marriage and communication and I was determined to be a better partner for Chris this time around. The first time we were married, I fell victim to the stress of life and responsibility, and I was not putting my best foot forward. The second time, I knew that I wasn't perfect—and I'm still far from it—but from that point on I was willing to work as hard as I needed to in order to be a better wife and mother.

In the heat of our breakup, we'd said many hurtful things to each other. The first thing we had to do when we came back together was to forgive each other for everything that had been said so that we could start fresh. And we promised that anytime we had a disagreement going forward we wouldn't turn to insults but would talk it out with respect for each other's feelings.

We got to a place where we could come back together and be the best for each other. We were officially remarried about two years later.

This time we had a wedding at Orange Beach in Alabama, where we'd been renting a beach house for annual summer reunions with our aunts and uncles and cousins since Austin was just a couple of months old. These trips to the beach started out as gatherings of my dad's side of the family. Then my mom started coming with her sisters. Then Chris's family started renting a house there, too. It's become a big, chaotic, ridiculously fun annual family party.

One thing I love most about it is that all these incredibly different personalities come together and make memories. Chris's older sister Diane, for example, who works in administration at the Corsicana Independent School District and has a son, could not be more different from Chris. She's very reserved and careful. Chris is liable to jet off to Las Vegas at a moment's notice, but she has a typed itinerary for everything. All of these different people came together to share our joy.

These were the witnesses I wanted for our second—final!—wedding. There was no limo this time. My uncle, who is a pastor, married us on the beach in an intimate ceremony with just our family and a few close friends in attendance. Austin and Ally were by our sides, and they were so happy. Ally and I wore white dresses and Austin and Chris wore white shirts and khakis. The weather was beautiful and we hired someone to play music. We had food catered from Moe's Original Barbecue. Whereas the first time our party had been big and loud and boozy, this time it was small and quaint and quiet. We just wanted to make it official again. And after our vacation, we went back to our home.

This isn't to say we waved a magic wand and marriage became totally easy that very day. Our kids were still young and we had full-time jobs, so we certainly had a lot going on. But we promised one another that we would do a better job of communicating and we'd learn how to be there for each other. We know it's always going to be work, but because of what we learned from our divorce we've been much better at it this time around. I no longer get upset if Chris is taking a weekend trip with the guys. I make sure to spend time with the girls. We don't keep score with the chores, and if we feel that we need more help, we ask for it rather than seething.

And something else wonderful has happened: my divorced parents have become friends as time has gone by. My mom and my stepfather started dating each other pretty soon after the divorce and there was a lot of bad blood. For years, we had to throw separate birthday parties for the kids so my parents wouldn't have to be in the same room together. We'd have to invite my mom to one get-together, and then have another and invite my dad to that. A lot of families have to do that in the wake of a divorce that doesn't end well. While I know it means double presents for the kids, the downside is far greater.

Over the years, things between my parents got a lot better. Slowly we were able to have family gatherings where everyone was present at the same time and no one felt uncomfortable. And as everyone continued to be civil, they even became friends. My dad had a stroke five years ago, and my mom and my stepfather, John, both help us take care of him. If we have to take him to the emergency room, we can always count on my mom or John to come if we need them. John even goes and picks up my dad and takes him to get a haircut every few weeks. He'll take him to the store if he runs out of coffee. Once we realized the trip to the beach in Alabama was too far to drive with my dad, my mom and John started flying there with him.

When I look at how great things are now between my parents compared to how bad they were twenty years ago, I feel so much hope in humanity. More than anything else, my parents' reconciliation and mine with Chris showed me the tremendous power of communication. Chris and I had to learn to get over the pain we had caused each other, and we had to teach ourselves and each other how to share our feelings honestly and how to forgive.

Growing up, I didn't have perfect role models for how to make a marriage work. I didn't see a lot of communication between my parents, nor did I see them spending time together as friends and just hanging out. They attended certain social events together, but beyond that I didn't see two people who enjoyed each other's company. Chris and I had to create our own framework for a true partnership.

I realized that by actually talking about your feelings as they occur—even when you'd rather sweep them under the rug—you can avoid a lot of the misunderstandings that lead to resentment.

This also helped me as a coach, especially in dealing with college kids who wind up in online feuds. If you say, "Well, let's just sit down and talk about it," very often something that's been simmering for weeks can be resolved in minutes. When we actually have a face-to-face conversation with someone with whom we have a beef, the problem often vanishes.

On the cheer team, I try to be extremely clear with everyone. Sometimes it's necessary to pull people aside and have a tough conversation with them. Maybe they are on mat but not quite getting the job done, so I have to let them know that their position may be in jeopardy if some skill doesn't get better. This is never a fun conversation. I like to encourage people, so having to tell someone that they aren't doing something up to par is tough. I am direct enough in the conversation so that they are clear regarding my expectations. I try to be honest about what the outcome could be if they don't improve. At the same time, I make sure that they know that I believe in their ability to turn it around.

Whatever it is, it must be addressed. Otherwise, these things can spread. I have found that most people want to improve and grow.

They just need direction and, quite honestly, sometimes they need to be told what is missing. That is how I am, too. If I am told that I have done something wrong or need to do something better, it eats at me. Being bothered by it is exactly what prompts me to change. I work hard to make the bad feeling go away.

I make sure I tell people about my divorce and remarriage, because I don't believe in feeling shame for failing. Everyone fails at some point in their lives. And in this case I believe the problems Chris and I worked through wound up being a blessing. That was the moment when I said, "You know what? I can't control everything that's going on right now, but I can control myself. I'm going to work on myself and be the best that I can be for my family."

Thankfully, that's exactly what I did.

Chris and the kids and I all have to communicate with one another about what we need. We have to support one another to live our dreams, to be good teammates.

Just as in any coaching job, I'm gone a lot. I have to be at not only all of our practices but all the other teams' games. We cheer volleyball, soccer, basketball, and football. The football team plays almost every Saturday in the fall. And we're not there just from the time the game starts until it ends. We have to be there an hour before the game starts. And if the game is out of town, we have travel time on top of that.

We don't do overnight trips very often, unless we go to camp or Daytona, but there are a lot of little trips where it's still far enough that you have to stop for food. So if it's an out-of-town game, I'm gone all day long. We usually practice every afternoon Monday through Friday plus two weeknights during the season, so that's a couple of nights a week that I'm away from home. But we've learned as a family to all be on the same page, to realize that my job is good for all of us.

Every job involves a give-and-take. And this job comes with some great flexibility. I have several weeks off, which means I never had to send my kids to day care in the summer. I have to give up a lot of weekends and evenings to be a coach, but I can give my children every summer. For us, it's been worth it. And nothing makes me prouder than seeing my kids and husband in the stands at our games cheering on my squad.

You can accomplish more in every aspect of your life when you know how the people around you are feeling and when you express your own feelings to them. Learning to communicate with Chris made me a better coach. My ability to communicate well with my cheerleaders made us a stronger team.

These days I make sure I am extremely clear. I also want to hear from people directly. I like to include the team in decision-making—especially anything involving skills. After all, they are the ones doing the physical work. There's something about that, I think, that's easily missed in relation to leadership—how important it is to bring everybody into the decisions you're making. Everyone on a team needs to have ownership. Not only do you want a good leader, you want good leaders on the team. You need to make everyone (whether in a marriage or in a squad) feel appreciated. If people don't feel appreciated, they tend to start feeling angry. And then they don't want to give 100 percent of themselves.

I married Chris for the second time twelve years ago. Now our children are out of the house and it's just us. Chris's career is going well and I've had opportunities in the past year I never could have imagined. We're able to be there for each other without the resentment we had all those years ago, and to support one another. At every turn my life has taken this past year, Chris has been there cheering me on.

10

YOUR DOUBT IS MY FUEL

Several years ago at the annual National Cheerleaders Association summer camp at Southern Methodist University, I was at a coaches' meeting about college nationals. The speaker was explaining how the intermediate division was a way for teams to build their programs, but that the end goal was for them to move up to the advanced division.

Since my team already competes at the advanced division level, I was casually listening without much thought to what was being said. But during this discussion one of the intermediate-division coaches in attendance mentioned Navarro College. I perked up to see how I might be a part of this conversation. It turned out the coach was saying, "If I had talent like what they have at Navarro College, I could compete at the advanced level!"

I thought to myself, *That sounds like a compliment. We're an example of excellence! How nice.*

The conversation continued. Within minutes, a different coach brought up Navarro College—then another coach and then another. Each made similar points about "Navarro talent" as they talked about recruiting and the admission pool.

After a few minutes of this, I found myself growing annoyed. No one meant any harm. As I said before, it was a compliment. And yet, I felt as though they were dismissing all my years of hard work plus the many hours of practice the team had just put in to prepare for the camp.

Finally, I had to say something. I love my colleagues. They are wonderful friends of mine. But I had to tell them that there is no magical "Navarro talent pool."

"We weren't born good. We worked hard to become good," I said. "I've hardly slept because we've been doing three practices a day. That's why they look good and prepared. They put in the time."

The conversation that day revealed a kind of belief that can stand in the way of success. Anybody's capable. You don't have to take over the talented team. You don't even have to have that much talent to start with. You can make your own dynasty. Each year I have new people coming onto my team and I'm taking a gamble on every single one of them. I may have been looking to recruit you for years. I may have met you for the first time at tryouts. Who knows? But at the end of the day, when you get here and I'm actually working with you, that's where success comes from. Rarely can anyone get away with just talent. And it took years for me to get the program to where it is.

I meet my new team for the first time each year about six days before we go to that NCA summer camp. Many of these young adults are fresh out of high school. They have zero college experience and have never been through the kind of practices we run at Navarro. To say we work hard for those six days is an understatement. We are usually putting in three practices daily and preparing for camp with new skills, learning routines, and doing full outs. It is exhausting for all of us, to say the least.

So there I am in this meeting, completely worn out from about twenty practices straight in the span of less than a week with a new group of students, just trying to survive until camp is over. Was all of that work and sacrifice I just put in leading up to our camp performance being portrayed as nothing more than luck? Did my fellow coaches really think that year after year I was just given a group of amazing cheerleaders and all I had to do to get them ready for cheer camp was load them onto the bus? Or that they could simply put on Navarro uniforms and turn out an amazing show at camp?

This doesn't just happen. I'd love it if our school admission letters also bestowed superpowers on our kids, but they do not. Every student on that team—some of whom come in with only the most basic skills—works insanely hard to learn new difficult skills so that they can compete at the highest level.

Beyond that, I was sitting there in that little room full of coaches and all I could think about were those first years coaching. I definitely started at the bottom. I was thrown into the job mid-season, handed keys to the gym and to a fifteen-seat passenger van. Then I was introduced to the fourteen members of the team. They were just days away from competing at the NCA Collegiate National Championship. It was December 1994, and the competition wasn't yet held in Daytona; it was still being held in Dallas over Christmas break. I met the team and watched them practice, and we headed to Dallas.

I had no idea what I was doing. Several of the team members were older than I was! I had never coached. I'd never driven a giant van, never even driven in downtown Dallas. On top of everything, it snowed that weekend of the first competition. I got them to and from the event safely, but I didn't do much more to help them besides clap as I watched them lose.

During those first years, I didn't feel like the people I worked for understood the sacrifices I was making to build the cheer program. They didn't understand the value that we brought to the school or the athletic department. Compared with other sports, I was never given equal funding, equipment, or respect. I fought tooth and nail for everything I got and often went home feeling angry.

I got the sense that the administration at the time did not expect too much from me. I would go to some department to take care of something and they'd address me as if I were a student. Now that I'm middle-aged, I would love to be mistaken for a student! But back then, I would think to myself, *I can't wait until I'm older. I can't wait until I have more experience under my belt and can command the respect that comes with that.*

When I started coaching I was just twenty-two. But if someone in the business office talked to me like I was a dumb cheerleader who didn't know how to balance a budget I would push back. I was exceedingly careful with my budget. Having someone doubt that would make me mad. But I also believe in killing people with kindness. Every job is easier if you do it with a good attitude.

So I'd simply say to these doubters: "You'll never have to talk to me about my budget. I have a finance degree. I'll always be on point with my budget." And I'd think, *You go ahead and talk to me like I'm a child who doesn't understand how money works. I'm going to smile, and I'm going to go do my job and I'm going to show you.* Then I would get back to work.

It would have been easy for me to succumb to low expectations and just do enough to get by (after all, there were no expectations of our squad in those early days). Thankfully, my competitive nature didn't allow me to do any less than my best. And eventually, once we started winning, cheer got the attention I believed we'd always deserved. In that situation, it took winning, but good leaders see passion and drive in others, and they reward potential as much as they do results.

Right away, my first year on the job, it was clear to me that our team was too small. My first order of business was to get more bodies into that gym. In the early days I didn't have a lot of people trying out, so I usually took all of the male candidates. But we still didn't have enough power, so I went into the weight room to recruit bigger boys who looked athletic. I even recruited a few of the girls' boyfriends.

And I kept growing the team. Year by year, we grew from four-teen to sixteen to twenty to twenty-four to twenty-six to twenty-eight. . . . This year, we had thirty-nine people on the team. Next year, my new team will have more than forty.

I also saw that we needed more practices. I added more workouts, more full outs. More work, period. I began to live and die by the score sheet. I memorized the rubric for which stunts score how many points, and I built a routine that gave us the best chance for the high-est score. People acted like I was crazy. At that time, cheerleading was more based on who could do the hardest partner stunts. But I knew that even though we might not have the most challenging stunts, if we hit every single category in the score sheet, we could win on points.

That's how I started, and I never gave up. It was hard, but I went ahead full force. I didn't say, "Oh man, I wish I had this amazing team," like some of those coaches were saying that day at the camp. I went in and built it myself. And when I got knocked down, I picked myself up and kept going. I knew that I wanted to build something great, and I sacrificed my time and energy to do exactly that.

So to be at that camp meeting hearing things like "If I had talent like Navarro" did not sit well with me. When nobody shows up for tryouts, are you just going to go, "Oh well, I'm just going to find another job where there's a better team"? No, you're going to find a way to make the team great, even if that means heading into the weight room and tapping kids on the shoulder.

One thing I've heard a lot from young people, especially women, is that they worry about being worthy. In business you often see this called impostor syndrome. I've been lucky in my life not to suffer from self-doubt, and maybe in part it's because I tend not to care what other people think of me. Honestly, my friends will tell you I was probably shorted a bit in the sensitivity department when I was born. My friend Jeri says that I'm a stereotypical man, just like her husband. I don't listen to stories very well. I don't pay attention to details. I don't think beyond the situation at hand.

She's right that I'm not very sensitive. It's not easy to hurt my feelings. In my career I've certainly had experiences that anyone might consider sexist. People have failed to have enough faith in me because I'm a woman. But these moments barely register, because I don't pay very close attention to things that don't interest me. And anyone who doesn't recognize that I can take on the world just doesn't interest me.

Confrontations don't intimidate me. I will be polite, but I will hold my ground. If I have something I'm passionate about, or I know I'm right about, I won't back down. If anything, I can be over-confident. The world throws enough obstacles our way. We don't need to add more by doubting ourselves.

This is especially important for women. We can't see ourselves as less powerful just because we're women. When you see yourself that way, then you might start to act like weakness is a possibility. And it's not.

When it comes to women friends of mine or female cheerleaders who are struggling with impostor syndrome, I always say that we need to remind ourselves that in these situations what's at stake is not only our own lives and careers but also the quality of the work itself. If ever someone is trying to belittle you or take something away from you—you fight. Discrimination is straight-up wrong. Remember: you *deserve* to be there. You have so much to offer. If someone's insecurity or ignorance is keeping them from seeing your potential, that's their problem, not yours. We must not internalize their misunderstanding.

Over the years, plenty of men have said condescending things to me, but my attitude is usually: *You don't think I'm worthy of being here? And who are you again?* I'll go toe to toe with anyone who tries to dismiss me or anyone I love. While in my personal life I try to be more attentive to my family and friends, I think that in my business life my lack of sensitivity allows me to have the confidence I need.

I believe that sensitive people have an advantage in their personal lives. They are by nature more thoughtful and attuned to others' needs. But when it comes to business or work, I worry for the ultrasensitive.

I love short answers, and if I can reply yes or no to a question, that's as far as I'll go. I've been told that's intimidating. I think women in particular are encouraged to couch their direct answer in extras like "Well, I'm not sure, of course, but I think . . ." or "Just going out on a limb here, and I'm sorry if I'm overstepping, but . . ."

Who has time for all that? Let's get to the point. I'm a black-and-white-type person. I'm busy and don't really see a need to add the fluff when I can just state the facts. I know that sensitive people may read judgment or coldness into it. My more sensitive cheerleaders often overanalyze conversations or actions. But over time they get used to the way I talk and they learn not to take it personally.

There is tremendous power in being able to take criticism without crumbling. I understand that young people often have trouble with this. They want to be perfect from day one. But nobody ever is. What will give you the edge over all the other not-perfect people around you is the ability to listen to feedback and make adjustments. I'd much rather coach someone who's raw but humble and eager to learn than someone who's more accomplished but thinks they have it all figured out.

I've tried to meet the sensitive members of my team halfway. I've worked on my shortness and tried to add more conversation to replies, but it's not my preferred way of communicating.

If you're sensitive and find yourself wondering why someone's speaking abruptly, remember that it's very rarely got anything to do with you. I know it's hard to brush things off so easily when that's not your nature, but I believe it's worth asking yourself if it might be what it looks like: that the person saying yes or no means that and nothing more. Cheerleaders on my team who early in the season spend hours analyzing an innocent reply, non-reply, or even a look taken the wrong way eventually learn not to waste their time and to take what I say at face value.

And they learn to appreciate how blunt they can be with me without my being offended. You can be very direct with me and I won't get upset. If anything, I'll use criticism as motivation. I need to do that better? Sure! Let's try harder! Something in a routine isn't working? Good to know! We can fix it without hemming and haw-ing. Let's keep it professional.

When I'm at work, I'm not there to be social. It's not that I don't have friends on campus, but when I'm there, I'm working. I'm either in practice or I'm in my office taking care of scheduling. I'm busy. It's business. I stay in my bubble. I don't interact very much. My office is off by itself. And I don't want to hear anyone's doubts or negativity unless it's productive.

The dynasty that we have grown at Navarro College did not just happen overnight. It took years for me to build and it took a lot of failures for me to learn and grow from. Sometimes in those early years I would feel beaten down because it was so hard to be all things to all kids. But I made sure I brought determination, grit, resiliency, and the desire to keep going no matter how hard it got. I looked at every failure as an opportunity to get better. Nothing motivates me more than failing at something. Nothing fires me up more than someone doubting me. Nothing makes me work harder than being counted out. I live for the challenge.

I said something to my fellow coaches about this at the cheer camp that day. I told them that they, too, could build their own amazing programs. It just takes time, commitment, and never giv-ing up. I also told them that in my experience the last thing a coach should be thinking about is the other teams. The way I run our program is with the belief that it doesn't matter what anyone else is doing. You can't play defense in cheerleading. All we can worry about is ourselves.

We all need to go out there, work the hardest that we can, and prepare the best routine that we can to the best of our ability. It's a subjective sport. People will always judge it based on opinion. It's not football, where if you cross the line you automatically get six points. All we can do is know that we've done our best, that we've put it all out there. If we prepare and we put on a great performance, then whatever the end result is, it really is success.

When I first started, other teams sometimes treated us badly because we were seen as beneath them. Now sometimes we're seen as so elite that we must have some sort of secret advantage. But all along we've always been the same—tireless workers. And the more people count us out, the harder we fight.

11

WHEN YOU GET DISTRACTED IS WHEN YOU HIT THE FLOOR

One evening this past spring after I got home from work I was in the kitchen cooking dinner when my phone buzzed. Stirring sauce with one hand, I picked up my phone with the other. I saw that I had a DM on Instagram from Dillon. Dillon Brandt is on the cheer team. He'd attached a link to an article about *Cheer* and the other big docuseries of the moment, *Tiger King*. The DM read: "Hey, we made the same article! I feel blessed." The article's title was "*Tiger King* Has a Connection to *Cheer*, Because the Netflix Universe Is That Small."

As I opened the fridge and pulled out ingredients, I wrote back, "Ha. WTH is that?" I'd just watched *Tiger King* and found it to be equal parts wacky and impossible to look away from. It was a world that I didn't know existed. It made me want to go to Garvin County, Oklahoma, to see Joe Exotic's place in person.

Dillon wrote back: "No clue. One of my alums sent it to me."

These kids today. I shook my head while I set the table and thought, *Dillon, everything is not about you.*

"They're talking about that Dillon guy from *Tiger King*," I texted back as I took a pot off the stove.

"That's me. LOL," he wrote.

Why is Dillon thinking this article is about him? I thought. *He's getting a swelled head.* "No, Dillon," I said. "This is not about you. They are talking about that Dillon guy from *Tiger King.*"

And he said, "That's me," with a dead-face emoji.

I said, "The Dillon guy they are talking about is married to Joe Exotic! He cheered at SFA!"

And he said, "It's still me. LOL."

As I called Chris to the table, I felt exasperated with Dillon. *Why is he still talking about this* Tiger King *article like the article is about him when it's about—*

Sitting down to eat, I realized: I'd been DM'ing not with Dillon Brandt, my cheerleader, but with Dillon Passage from *Tiger King.*

I wrote: "OMG. I thought you were Dillon Brandt."

Fortunately, Dillon Passage thought it was very funny (as did Dillon Brandt, when I told him about it later).

As a student, Passage had been a cheerleader at Stephen F. Austin State University, a midsize liberal arts school in Nacogdoches, Texas. For years, Navarro did a pre-competition "show-off" performance at SFA every year when we were gearing up for Daytona. A show-off is a performance before a competition—basically a dress rehearsal. The drive to SFA is about three hours east, so once we started doing show-offs at Southern Methodist University, which is an hour north, we stopped going to SFA. But evidently one year when we were still going to SFA, Dillon Passage was on their team, which meant we performed in the same arena.

I tell this story because every time I try to do a few things at once—in this case, making dinner while texting—I do everything distractedly and screw up one thing or the other or both. The stakes in this case were very low—the Dillons and I got a good laugh out of it—but in the cheer world, being distracted can lead to serious injury. At all times, to stay safe, you need to know what part of the routine you are in and focus on that. If you're distracted or trying to do someone else's job rather than your own, you're putting yourself and others in danger.

The first part of staying focused on your job is knowing what your job is. In a cheer routine, everyone has a distinct part to play, and in assembling our pyramid in particular I do a lot of work trying to figure out how to help everyone shine.

There are so many analogies here to business and to life. Everyone assembles a team differently. I don't go by the old-school rule, which is that you always build a team around partner stunts. That's never quite worked for my teams, so I just do me.

When building a team, I'm looking for a certain number of young men who are going to be great stunters—meaning they throw the girls up in the air. Then I have some guys I call tumblers, who have elite tumbling skills. Usually they're a little smaller than the stunters. Every once in a while you'll have someone who is the best of the best in all skill sets, but most of my kids have areas of specialization.

Usually most of the girls are flyers—the ones who get tossed through the air and put up on shoulders—who also do basic to elite tumbling. But I do take some girls who aren't flyers if they're really good tumblers. When we're competing, we need those tumbling points, too. When building pyramids, we have what we call mid-layers—the girls who are standing on the guys' shoulders and holding another girl on top of them. Obviously the top girls are usually the smallest girls, because they need to be held up by another girl. Our mid-layer girls are usually the stronger ones, often a little bit bigger, so that they can lift the tiny girls.

There are three ways to look at a routine: in the tumbling section, everybody is responsible for only themselves. They have to land on their feet. If they don't, they're the ones who messed up. When you're doing a partner stunt, there are two people and a spotter. Those three people have control over that part; nobody else on the team does.

With the pyramid, the entire team comes together. Everyone is involved: whether you're holding a shoulder stand or throwing a girl to the top, you have to do your job precisely—and only your job—or the whole pyramid can collapse.

In life, there are moments when doing a good job is just your responsibility or others when it is dependent on you and one or two other people. But there is always a time when you need the whole team. In those situations, any one person not carrying his or her own weight can bring the whole thing crashing down.

As the leader, I have to keep in mind that I have a place in the pyramid, too. I have to be the best coach I can for my team—laser-focused, strategic about placement, emotionally supportive—so they can do their best. And for me, during the season that means staying totally focused on cheerleading, with no distractions. Other people have hobbies. I have cheerleading for work and cheerleading for fun, too.

I've always been single-minded. When I was a college student at UT Austin, this made me pretty boring. I was solely focused on school. I think I went to Sixth Street—the stretch that has all of the bars and cool places to hang out—maybe twice. I lived with three of my friends from high school my first year. My two best friends were way more laid back than me. They would occasionally miss class and would have to listen to me nagging them like I was an overprotective mom. I'm sure they were ready to get rid of me.

After that, I moved into an apartment by myself. I liked having my quiet space and my structure. I joined the sorority Zeta Tau Alpha, which hosted a bunch of fun philanthropic events. I dated Chris and worked a bunch of jobs, but mostly I preferred staying home and studying.

I'm still a bit of a homebody when I'm not working. It's not that I don't enjoy hanging out with my friends, but I've never had much leisure time. I do like to read, but I don't even get to do that much unless it's the summertime. I think that's why I keep my circle of friends small and close. I'd rather have four quarters than one hundred pennies.

What I've come to realize is that cheer is my life, and I'm okay with that. You hear a lot about diversifying and side hustles, but I've found that staying focused on one thing for so many years has let me be the very best I can be at coaching.

This single-minded attention can benefit us in many areas of life. I encourage everyone to find their passion and then to fully throw themselves into it. For the best results, don't have too many things on your plate, because you won't be able to give your best to any one thing. Give yourself fully to the task at hand. When you're fully focused, you're a lot less likely to tumble off your pyramid, fail at your job, or scold a *Tiger King* spouse thinking he's somebody else.

12

BUILD A STRONG PYRAMID

The pyramid to me is the quintessential metaphor for life—all those perfectly rehearsed movements coming together in one seemingly impossible shape. All those minds concentrating on doing their part to create one incredible experience for the audience. The pyramid is a culmination of all our hard work—something so much more intricate and magical than any one person could accomplish on his or her own. When I see an expertly pointed toe and a chin jutting out in triumph at the perfect angle, fifteen feet in the air, I get goose bumps. To me, there is nothing more beautiful than the teamwork and attention that makes something like that possible.

I am always looking for new ways to make pyramids more exciting. To earn difficulty points, you have to have people thrown from the ground straight up to the top of the pyramid. But personally, I get bored to tears just watching the usual thing. Someone throws someone else up. They hit their mark at the top, then pop off and come back to the ground, then take an eight count, then get thrown back up to the top. Yawn.

If you watch our pyramids, they're different. We never stop moving. We're not coming off and then resetting and then going back up again like pistons. We're coming off something and going *right* into something else, and from every possible direction—flying in and out sideways, diagonally, from any wacky combination of angles. That's the style I've always loved. That's what we're known for: constant motion.

To help us compose the most complex pyramid possible, Andy and I start working on ideas in the fall. Andy Cosferent is one of my assistant coaches. He was an athlete on my team from the fall of 2012 to the spring of 2015. He's from Canada, and I first met him when a friend of mine brought him all the way down to Corsicana to check out Navarro. I remember that he didn't come prepared to do anything, so rather than put on the proper gear, he tumbled barefoot. I still put him on the team.

After graduating, he came back often and volunteered his time to help out with the team. In 2018, I was able to hire him as my part-time assistant coach. He travels around the world doing choreography and working with teams, but we made the job work with his schedule. We've been through a lot in a short amount of time. He was with me every step of the way while we filmed *Cheer*, and we did a whirlwind PR tour together after its release. He's become my right-hand man in planning each year's pyramid.

Throughout the fall semester, Andy and I come up with all of our skills, and we pull together all our ideas for the partner stunt section, pyramid, and basket tosses (in which one cheerleader is thrown in the air by a few people with interlocking hands). The goal is always to have all those elements mostly set before we leave for Christmas break. We don't usually have all the pyramid elements done, but we finish it right when school starts back. Then it's time to call a choreographer, a freelancer from outside the school, for help putting it all together.

When the choreographer arrives, we present our work. We show him the pyramid. We show him the partner stunt sequence. We show him basket tosses. And then Andy and I sit down with him and we talk about what order we'd like based on what's physically possible.

In constructing the routine, Andy and I might need to put a tumbling section first, for example, because it's harder and otherwise the tumblers might be too tired by the time it comes around. We get that all mapped out and then the choreographer leaves.

The next day, he comes back full of ideas for how to make the transitions seamless. He'll say: "Right after the opening, this is a good skill to go straight into because then you'll create the best showcase for your best tumbling routine."

The choices are aesthetic and also strategic. You want to maximize every single moment, and you want it to look as fluid as possible. And by the time we're done, we've made every split second count in our two minutes fifteen seconds. Then it's just a matter of going full out on that plan over and over and over again—and over and over some more. And for the first however many times, it's probably going to fall apart.

I will say that the number one thing that makes a routine is confidence—the confidence of every single person in their ability to hit their marks and ace their position.

You may have noticed by now that confidence hasn't often been a challenge for me. Ever since I was a little girl, I've always had a weird belief that I can do anything I want to do and be anybody I want to be. Growing up, at my pediatrician's office, I'd think, *That person's a doctor! Why couldn't I be one, too?*

A certain amount of confidence is important. To be a cheerleader, you need to be able to imagine yourself at the top of the pyramid—smiling, hip cocked to the side, chin up—or at the bottom, holding up your teammates as if you were as strong as an oak tree.

Does my own level of hyper-confidence lead to embarrassment sometimes? Sure.

When I was in fourth grade, my friend had a piano at her house and she taught me how to play a simplified version of "Yankee Doodle." Leaving her house that day having mastered the task, I thought, *I'm the best musician there is!* And so I signed up to play two—not just one, but two—songs at the school Christmas program.

Now, I did not know how to play the piano *at all.* I didn't even have a piano in my home. And yet this taste of it gave me the confidence that I could certainly learn to play multiple Christmas carols. Well, of course I did not learn how to play anything. I stayed home from school that day to hide my shame. What kind of ridiculous confidence does someone need to actually sign up to play *two Christmas songs* with no experience?

When I played girls' soccer for a season my senior year of high school, I had no idea what I was doing. I had never played soccer in my life, but I loved it because it was so physical. Once, I got the ball and ran all the way down the field. I thought I had scored a goal and I looked back, elated, but everybody was just watching me, because the whole time I was offside (meaning I was ahead of the ball and thus in violation of the rules, so nothing I did counted). I didn't even know what offside was!

If you are wondering at this point how I could be a senior on a varsity sport, not even know the rules, and actually be in the game playing—well, that is a good question. I wonder the same. We had actually just started the girls' soccer program that season, so it didn't take much experience to make the team. I was fast and competitive, which I'm sure is the only reason I was able to get playing time.

I still say that failures like that are a small price to pay for taking risks. Confidence is essential in being successful at something as daunting as a pyramid. If you don't believe in yourself, then you can't expect others to believe in you. If that is something that you struggle with, then work on it. Every. Single. Day. Literally mat-talk yourself. When I am nervous about something or unsure of myself, I talk out loud and give myself a pep talk. I take deep breaths and imagine myself doing whatever the task is. I visualize myself killing it!

When I was packing to go to Los Angeles for *The Ellen DeGeneres Show* I was thinking about how frightening it was to do an interview on national television. I started mat-talking myself right there, out loud: "You will be great! You are going to be talking about something that you love. Something you know inside and out. Yes, it will be scary, but *you can do this!*"

I walked out of that room with my suitcase packed and the firm conviction *I can do this!*

In the greenroom—packed with people—I was saying all this in my head because mat talk works. Later, as I waited to go onstage, I kept saying these exact same things over and over again. Until the second I stepped out on that stage, I was reassuring myself that I would be great. This kind of self-talk calms your nerves and gives you that extra sense of confidence and self-empowerment.

Once you let negative thoughts in, self-doubt can guarantee the demise of your dream. As I've said, personally, I don't struggle with confidence, but I do have moments when I'm doing something new and doubt can linger in my mind. I attack it head-on by filling myself with positive energy and thoughts. The greater your doubt, the more you must tell yourself that you can do it, you belong, and you will succeed. Tell yourself these things again and again. Feel embarrassed that you are talking to yourself? That's just a sign that you need to say it all more!

Your mind is a powerful tool; it can make or break you. Your attitude is up to you alone. No one else should ever be able to get inside your head and control your thoughts. Be kind to yourself. Lift yourself up. And, most importantly, love yourself.

I know a lot of *Cheer* viewers felt very invested in Lexi Brumbach, a phenomenal tumbler with bleach-blond hair and a nose ring. The end of season one made some viewers think that she might be going back to various old ways. I'd like to reassure them that she wasn't. She is like a child of the '60s—so free-spirited that sometimes it seems she's about to levitate. (Her teammate Gabi Butler has that free-spirit vibe, too, but at home she had the structure that Lexi lacked.)

When Lexi arrived at Navarro, I knew that she'd been in physical altercations in the past—bad fights. I was prepared for her to be petty and confrontational. I was surprised by how quiet she was when she started on the team. She kept to herself, never said much. She'd never been in a program where there was so much emphasis on accountability and hard work. And although she'd been on good teams, she'd never won anything. Navarro presented a huge difference in structure, expectations, and work ethic. If you slack off at all, people are going to be on you. The team members don't want to disappoint me or one another. They believe, as I do, that to whom much is given, much will be required. If people show faith in you, your confidence grows.

I think Lexi was looking for the place where she fit in when she was a teenager, and she made some bad choices. But cheerleading became her safe space and gave her the structure that she was missing. Navarro took that even further and gave her goals to reach. It gave her expectations for herself. As a result, I have seen her confidence soar.

When Lexi realized that she truly belonged at Navarro, she found her bearings. She's unbelievably driven, and her teammates saw it right away. She'll leave everything she has out there on the floor. And when she realized people noticed it and would push her, she thrived. Lexi became one of the greatest assets to our team. We are all capable of redemption. No matter how many times you've screwed up and no matter what your past is, you deserve great things.

When you're dealing with athletes who are talented and motivated, they push each other. When you have some of the best skills in the gym, what new challenge can you find for yourself? On the team, I see everyone at some point or another notice the person next to them doing something and think, *I wonder if I can do that, and do it even better.*

You have to find motivation wherever you can. Often what helps most is surrounding yourself with people who embody what you want to become and who help you grow into the best version of yourself. You need people cheering you on, pushing you forward, and helping you see a future in which your dreams come true.

Building a championship culture, a community, with shared standards of excellence, is a lot like building a successful pyramid. They both take planning, hard work, putting in the time, guidance from the top, and contributions from every member.

We've built a championship culture at Navarro, so expectations are high. Doing your job, being committed no matter the obstacles, is what makes a champion. And if you are in a competitive field and you don't have that drive, someone else will take your spot. To make it, you have to be ready to work harder than you've ever worked.

When kids come into my program, there's a lot asked of them—not just at practice, but even when they're just out and about. They are expected to behave themselves in a certain way and be ambassadors for the school. We do a lot of community service. Our president, Dr. Fegan, always says the special thing about community colleges is the word *community* because it helps our town rally around the college, and this mutual support makes both the school and its surroundings more special.

To give back to the community, we do a lot of different things throughout the year—we give pep rallies at other schools and make appearances at local businesses, parades, and community events, hospitals, and assisted-living homes. I believe it's good for the people the team spends time with; it's also good for the team. Spending time with the elderly and with kids in a cancer ward gives them perspective on how fortunate they are in their own lives and how much of a gift it is that their bodies are so healthy and strong.

One of my favorite community service programs is our mentoring work through the local YMCA. Cheerleaders are paired up with mentees from a local elementary school. These kids are chosen by their teachers because they are at higher risk for bad outcomes. The cheerleaders visit with the kids once a month and find fun activities to do together.

It feels good to give back, whether that means paying special attention to kids who otherwise don't get a lot of attention or making people smile at a particularly exciting performance at an event. Doing for others without expecting anything in return is one of the best things you can do, no matter who you are. Every year I see my kids recognize this—that serving others is a blessing for those who receive but maybe even more so for those who give.

In my program, there's also a very high expectation of how hard cheerleaders are going to work: *very hard*. Some people make the team, but they're really not cut out for the program. They're not a fit for that kind of self-discipline and hard work. They're not happy because they're not used to (and they don't *want* to get used to) that push. They don't make it through. They quit. They get kicked off. They're not willing to give up their social life or personal time or whatever else. So when you are talking about a program that has a championship culture, it must be made up of people who are here to do the job. Not everybody's cut out for it. When it comes to making it to that top level, it's just a fact: some people won't make it through.

Meanwhile, the successful people are willing to sacrifice. I'm not asking anyone else to do what I wouldn't do. I sacrifice time with my family. I sacrifice downtime for myself and recreational time with friends. There are events I don't attend because I'm working. But if I'm committed to something, I'm going to do whatever it takes to be successful in that arena.

Those are the successful people in *every* area of life: the ones who are willing to sacrifice and go that extra mile that the average person's not willing to.

When I see some people on the team, I know by the look in their eyes that I can count on them no matter what. It's not anything that's said. It's literally a characteristic of certain people. The way we prepare physically and mentally on my team, everyone is set up to learn to fill that role. If they are in a routine and things start falling apart, I can count on them to finish and push through and not fall apart with it.

One team member who exemplifies this spirit is tumbler Dillon Brandt (the Dillon *not* on *Tiger King*). I've coached him for a long time, so I know him really well. I've seen him in action many times. Again and again I've seen how fast he thinks. His role in a partner stunt is to be what we call the spotter—someone on the ground who keeps an eye out for any potential problems during a stunt or a tumble. Spotters rescue routines all the time, and they prevent untold injuries. And I would put money on Dillon a hundred out of a hundred times to keep any stunt in the air, no matter what is going wrong.

Some people overcompensate for a mistake, like a teetering foot on the pyramid, and grab too hard, knocking everything over in the attempt to stabilize a wobble. But Dillon always knows the exact right amount of effort to make. He's able to keep smiling and stay steady so no one watching can even tell there was a mix-up. In a pyramid someone might be teetering on a shoulder stand and then you see Dillon's arm shoot up as if to say, *No, you're not coming down.* And they don't come down. I call that smart cheerleading.

It's always interesting to watch a bunch of different teams, because you're going to see some of the same mistakes and how differently people handle them. Sometimes you can barely tell there was a mistake. That's how good some teams are. They can do something that's really off and you don't know, because they just never missed a beat. Others crumble at the first false move.

When we were in Daytona competing in the 2019 nationals, our tumbler Austin Bayles injured his ankle during competition, right in the middle of our routine. The music stopped and we had to clear the stage. Then we had to regroup quickly and try it again with a reconfigured team. We went through it a few times and then we had to get back out there. This put La'Darius Marshall in a tight spot. He and Austin were opposites in the dance portion of the routine. They were supposed to mirror each other. With no help from anyone else, La'Darius came up the middle and made up his own dance all the way through to the end. He never missed a beat.

That do-or-die spirit is what makes someone irreplaceable on a team, and that's what builds championship culture. That's what I always tried to be during my own cheer days. Even an injury wouldn't keep me from the floor if there were any way at all I could keep cheering.

Once, in seventh grade, I was riding a neighbor's moped. I was trying to show off in front of some boys, so I was going faster than I needed to be. Then I reached the end of a street where you have to turn one way or the other and I couldn't slow down fast enough. In a split-second decision, I just shut my eyes and went straight into a tree. I don't think any option would have been a good one, but the tree definitely was not a winning choice. I broke my wrist.

I didn't let my injury hold me back when it came to cheerleading, though. I still did as much tumbling as I could with one arm, running and flying with my cast on. In high school, too, I injured my wrist. I got a metal wrist brace so that I could continue to tumble and stunt on it while it healed. Where there's a will, there's always a way. And that's the spirit I look for in my cheerleaders. We all have to own our place in that pyramid or it won't stay up.

13

KEEP GOING UNTIL YOU GET IT RIGHT— AND THEN KEEP GOING UNTIL YOU CAN'T GET IT WRONG

A lot of us say this about cheerleading: *Most of the time it's not fun.* It's hard. It's exhausting. You're putting your body through all this pain and hard work and long hours of working out. And we do it all for these brief moments of success. Whether it's winning a championship, mastering a skill, or having a successful full out in practice—those moments of success are exhilarating. That's why we keep coming back and putting in the hours.

But before there are those moments of success, there are so many instances of getting it wrong. Failure is an absolute necessity for us to grow. I always tell the team: "Fail hard, so we know what to fix!" When you don't fail, sometimes you get complacent. Even those people who are fighters, who work really hard, can settle in and get a little lazy. But when you fail, it reenergizes you and keeps you motivated.

I am a big believer in the old saying that failure is where the learning happens. Not that it feels good.

We had a seven-year winning streak from 2009 to 2015. Then we lost in 2016. That one was rough. So in 2017 I returned to Daytona having worked my butt off. The team had been practicing nonstop. Nothing was going to get in our way. We even had perfected one of the most difficult things we'd ever tried: five pike-open double basket tosses. That's the hardest basket toss that you can do. A pike-open double basket is when the person is thrown into the air and they go into a piked flipping position and then immediately do two spins to finish the rotation. The last year that these baskets were legal was 2018. The new safety guidelines now limit our basket tosses to certain skills and only allow for one flip and one spin.

At that time, I think only one other university had even competed with five pike-open double baskets in competition. And for a junior college to do it was already unexpected. Thanks to the two-year turnover in the team, we were at a disadvantage when it came to developing the toughest skills, because we were always dealing with new kids.

We spent endless hours working on these difficult skills. We had a *beautiful* routine. We were in first place with the highest score of the whole competition after prelims, the important rounds of judging before the big event on the main stage. And then at finals the team made two mistakes that were both total flukes.

When I say *fluke*, I mean no one could have predicted these mistakes. If someone was questionable in a skill, I would have changed it. But no one had ever made these mistakes in practice. Then, in the finals, disaster struck twice! One girl who was doing a tumbling skill over-rotated, meaning she had too much power on her landing and fell backward. Then another girl who had a specialty tumbling pass through the center of the stage also fell. Later she said it was because she felt like the mat was shorter there than it was back in our practice space. She mistakenly thought that if she took up all the space she usually did, she'd flip right off the front of the stage. And so she tried to change her tumbling mid-flip, which is not a good idea *ever*. And she landed on her side. It looked crazy.

We lost, obviously, because we had two deductions. I thought our overall score might be so high because of the difficulty level that the fluke errors wouldn't make us lose, but they did. For all of us, it was a tough, tough, tough loss, because we had done everything right: we'd selected a difficult routine and prepared thoroughly—we did it all. And still, we lost.

As we were getting on our bus after landing at the airport post-defeat, I thought, *Can I just put a cap and sunglasses on and not look at anybody?* I literally didn't want to make eye contact with anybody for weeks.

Cassius, our wonderful bus driver, did not sugarcoat it. He said he'd been watching the livestream along with a bunch of other people at the college in the Navarro auditorium. Cassius has worked here forever, and he's the biggest athletics supporter at the college. He drives the volleyball team and the softball team. And when we climbed aboard the bus he said: "Man, I can't believe y'all lost."

I said, "Yeah, I know. Sorry."

"It was like a funeral at the college," he said.

"Well, thanks for pepping me up," I said. "I'll just get on the bus now and sink into my depression."

Of course, if people tried to make me feel better I didn't like that either. I'm not going to lie; once I was even rude to one of our coaches who tried to console me after a loss, bless his heart.

He said, "Good job!"

I snapped back, "No, it wasn't a good job! Don't lie about it!"

Still, you should never give the people on your team who make mistakes a hard time. It could be anyone, and it's already such a heavy weight on them. Right after something happens, emotions are high. There are always people on the team who are mad that you messed up. I feel for the people who mess up, because it's a burden. You could carry it around forever: "Oh, well, that year we lost because of . . ." You become known for that mistake. I try to console them, saying that no one blames them. I say it as many times as they need to hear it: we are all a team and all in this together. If one person falls, we all fall. If one person succeeds, we all do.

The loss in 2017 was a reminder to me that I can only control so much. We did everything we could. And the year had been a hard one already, because just a couple of weeks before Daytona, I had to kick one of my on-mat performers off the team. He'd gotten arrested for having marijuana in his car. We have a zero-tolerance policy for drugs in the cheer program. These cheerleaders are role models for the community. I know no one is perfect by any means, and I'll give lots of second chances, but I can't when it comes to drugs. The rules are the rules.

After we lost that stunter, I spent an entire practice teaching an alternate his part. We finally got to where we said, "Okay, let's do it full out." That's when I realized this new kid didn't have the stamina to do the old routine. So we took a break. When we came back, we put in a different alternate, rearranged things, moved people around.

The next day we were supposed to do a show-off at another college with other teams. We usually do show-offs for a large crowd. But in this case we weren't ready for the public to see it. Instead, we decided to practice that day and have our own private show-off the following day. We invited our alumni—whoever could come down for the day. They would be a friendly crowd but also not afraid of offering specific critiques. That went okay. The alumni pointed out what we needed to improve and what they thought was working well. And they gave the team a boost of optimism and hope just in time. A week later we went to Daytona.

That last-minute change had caused a lot of turmoil. We had worked so hard. It was a tough, tough loss that year. I don't really cry that much, especially about work, but I shed tears. I was sad for a good month. I have never felt defeated after a loss, only disappointment. But for those few weeks, I felt completely defeated. And then finally I said to myself, *Okay, it's time for you to get over this. You've been sad long enough.* And I got to work on the next season's team full steam ahead.

A lot of people try to avoid things that are hard, but if you try to avoid the hard things, they don't go away. They're out there, waiting for you. I've seen people turn to crutches—become dependent on alcohol or drugs—because they're trying to avoid feeling something that doesn't feel good. But if you do that, you never make it to the other side.

When I went through my divorce there were days that I felt hopeless, frightened, and full of despair. I allowed myself to feel it. I'd say to myself, *I'm just going to sit here and I'm going to cry. I'm going to feel so sorry for myself and I'm going to get every single emotion out. Then I'm going to get up, and I'm going to move forward and take on the next day.*

If you don't let those emotions out, if you don't feel all those feelings, they'll fester. If I'm really angry, I might type up a really ugly email and then not send it. And as I read it over a few times, I find the anger melting away, like a knot being massaged. I'm able to let go of that anger without actually causing a problem. Or if I tell the same indignant story five times, by the sixth time it's stopped being infuriating and has started being funny. I've felt every emotion, let it all out, and moved on. It's like running—I hate it when I'm doing it, but afterward I feel so much better.

Healing emotionally is kind of like healing from an injury. You just have to allow yourself to experience what is uncomfortable, difficult, frustrating. When my kids are going through tough things, I say, "It's okay to be sad and it's okay to feel sorry for yourself. Just wallow in it for a moment, but don't stay there, because then it can become dangerous."

It takes strength to accept that it's time to really feel negative feelings. Then you've got to say: "I'm going to get up and I'm going to move forward. Not that I can't feel sad again in a couple of days, but right now I've got work to do."

In our culture, we react to problems by looking to fix them right away. Or if you have pain, it's: "Make the pain go away immediately!" And when we have a physical problem we tend to take care of it by dealing with the symptoms rather than the underlying cause.

When I was having neck issues, I went for adjustments and cortisone shots, but the only thing that actually worked long term was physical therapy. My physical therapist said, "When you get adjusted, you're just releasing a little air pocket or tension. That's going to make it feel better temporarily, but then it's going to come right back to that same spot. You have to learn how to strengthen your muscles and hold yourself in the right posture if you want it gone for good."

The only way out is through. Fight right through it. Feel the pain, feel the sadness. Get up and do it again. And guess what? Afterward you're stronger. There's an extra energy to competing the next time after you've failed. You sure don't ever want to feel that way again. In this way, every misstep is a gift. It doesn't feel like a gift at the time. It feels *terrible* at the time. But eventually it reveals its value.

In the gym, when we do our first full out for a routine, the expectation is not that we be perfect. It's that we be as successful as we can. We know that we have a long way to go to get our bodies in shape, to be at our very peak. It's a starting point, and you want to know what you need to work on. You want to go hard, but you begin by doing it in steps. There's a process to building up our stamina and strength, so that we're safe. You can't expect to do a routine full out and succeed every single time.

Sometimes we'll have a really bad full out. It looks terrible, mistakes are made, and people fall. It's a wake-up call. We say, "We need to check in and do better. If we get lazy, then we're definitely going to get beat." It motivates us to go back, to pump ourselves up. We often have some of the very best full outs right after the very worst ones.

We begin choreographing based on what we think we can do that will let us hit the most points on a score sheet. We always try to challenge ourselves and craft the routine to meet a very high standard. But as we practice it always gets tweaked and changed. Once you start going full out, you realize you might not have power left at the end to throw in that tumbling skill. We don't know that until we attack a routine head-on. We don't know until we try. If something's not working, we don't give up immediately. We find ways to tweak it so that we reach the outer limits of what we can do.

So we start going full out in sections, and with time and preparation, we realize, *Okay, we're ready to go full out completely.* Again, I don't expect the team to be perfect at this point. If they can't hit that tumbling in the middle of the routine when we go full out for the first time, I'm not worried about it. But as we start going full out more and more, that's when I start evaluating: *Okay, well, they've not hit that yet. I'm probably going to need to change it.*

I have it either written down or in my head: that's an area that I'm going to need to pay attention to. Maybe we'll take that person out altogether in that tumbling section, or maybe we'll make the skill an easier one, but we always want to craft a routine to the best of our ability. That takes trial and error.

We never just waltz into competition. We put all the work in beforehand so we know what our strengths are and where we need to make changes. Ultimately, the routine should look very easy and we should be able to do it without any mistakes, but of course it's incredibly challenging.

Here's what people don't realize about the rehearsal process: we *want* to fail as hard as we can in practice so we know what to amend and have a successful performance when it counts. That's why we practice so much. Anything that you practice, you improve in.

At one point in my life, I was terrified of speaking in front of big groups of people. Unfortunately, my job required it. Those first few times I had to get up in front of crowds, I shook and shook. I read from index cards I'd spend days trying to memorize. I prepared in the mirror. I prepared in front of my family. I tried breathing exercises. And what made the biggest difference was just having to do those speaking gigs over and over again until I was accustomed to them. I still got nervous, but I wasn't so afraid anymore. Eventually I came to almost enjoy speaking in front of crowds. Almost.

I learned anything is possible if you just attack it head-on and you don't die. Then every time after that it's a little easier. I try to make sure my cheerleaders always understand that: that the more they work, the easier things get, and that if they fail, they're closer to being in a place where it's hard to fail again.

Of all the championships we've won, the proudest moment I've ever had in competition was in 2019. You can see it on the show, but I don't know if you can tell how absolutely petrified I was when I saw Austin take that fall.

Competing is like running as fast as you can for two minutes fifteen seconds. It's such an incredibly difficult thing for the kids to stop in the middle of that kind of adrenaline rush and then return to that energy level a half an hour later. At the best of times, it's hard physically to do a routine full out twice back-to-back. It takes everything out of you. But add in those nerves? That pressure? Talk about a challenge!

When Austin fell, we had to go straight from the main stage back to the warm-up room. In a situation like that, you are flooded with emotions. You were just in front of thousands of people, leaving everything on the floor. You were putting every bit of energy you have out there. And halfway through the routine, you have to stop and press pause. And then you have this big low. Some of the kids were crying. They already felt defeated, because they thought, *Oh, there's no way we can come back from this.*

Right after the injury, I met them backstage. The moment I saw that fear on their faces I knew I had to hold it together if we were going to have any chance of salvaging the day. I tried to disguise my panic. "It's fine!" I told them, trying to smile. "We've got this!"

We were actually lucky, because the other teams were out on a lunch break. This gave us a few minutes in the warm-up area on our own with nobody else on the mats. Everything's kind of a blur looking back. It happened so fast, and we needed someone to fill in for Austin right away. There's no designated first alternate, because every person's role is unique. I looked around at everyone who could conceivably do what Austin did in the pyramid. My eyes settled on Alex Bouhuys, a freshman.

About a month before we went to Daytona, Austin had hurt his back and had to sit out for a couple of practices. I'd made Alex go in and do his part in the pyramid, but several weeks had passed since then. So I knew he probably didn't remember all the counts, but I knew he was capable. Alex couldn't do everything that Austin was doing in that routine, but he could get pretty close tumbling-wise. If we'd had more notice that Austin would need to be replaced in the finals, I might have chosen someone different. I would have been looking at everything Austin did in the routine and trying to make up for all the elements. For those who know the lingo, the moves in question were: a toe-full, a standing-two-to-full-full, a one-to-full. It's a lot to do! Plus, the person would need to hold a shoulder stand and the weight of the pyramid.

But all I cared about at that point was the pyramid. We had done several hundred reps of that pyramid. It was tough and it was a thing of beauty. Properly executed, it would earn us points in the higher range of the score sheet.

Like I said, everything we do is like putting a puzzle together. So if one person becomes injured, then I have to look around and see which person is going to be able to fill that particular spot.

The solution was to only have Alex come in on a couple of different parts that we needed to execute, but still, he had to know when to come in, when to come out, not to mention how not to be in anybody's way. In mere minutes we were trying to go through the pyramid, teach him the counts, teach him *everything*. I couldn't tell if it was even possible, but I knew that I had to pretend it was possible or we'd be sunk. I had to encourage them and keep them as positive and confident as possible, because I didn't want them to go out there scared. In twenty minutes, we walked through the pyramid choreography four times and we ran through the full routine twice.

I knew they needed to feel my calmness and be assured of my confidence in them. I told them that if anyone could overcome this and go back out there and hit this routine, it was them. We did not do all of those full outs all season for nothing. *This* was where their hard work, dedication, and relentless work ethic were going to come into play. This moment was theirs.

The truth is that my cheerleaders thrive in the face of adversity. You could have heard a pin drop as our time to return to the stage approached. Everyone was ready to tackle this problem, fight through it, do whatever we needed to do to get where we needed to be.

Looking them each in the eye, in the strongest mat-talk voice I could muster, I said, "We did not come this far just to come this far. I believe in you and YOU CAN DO THIS! Now go out there and do your job one section at a time. I love you guys!"

Then it was time to go. The team joined hands and recited the Serenity Prayer. And they headed back to the stage.

I wanted to believe that it would all be okay. I wanted to be sure. But honestly, I did not know that they had this. It was a lot to ask of anyone, much less rattled young people.

I got into position to watch the show and I prayed.

As they came onstage I was near tears. I was so impressed by their bravery and commitment. They were smiling huge smiles. They were ready to go full out. From the very first second they stepped onto that stage, they were on fire. Given the energy they brought into that second performance, I was not surprised that they hit the routine.

Yes, I could see open holes in formations where Austin belonged. I knew it wasn't as pristine as it would have been had we not had an injury. But it was still a really, really good routine and they nailed it. We had a lot of difficult skills and they went out there and hit them all a second time. To do that is mentally *and* physically tough, and every single one of those team members met the challenge.

It's hard enough to have months to prepare only to have it come down to one two-minute performance. But when you have less than half an hour to completely reconceive a routine, it's nearly impossible to perform well. I was so proud of them. And I saw their success as a true testament to the work ethic that we put into our practices. That is the thing that really sets us apart: our preparation for competition.

Technically, we weren't going to be judged on the section of the routine they'd already done before Austin's injury stopped the show, but you're always being judged. And you have to do the routine full out again from beginning to end. Otherwise it's not fair to be able to just do the end and not be as tired as you normally would be. Besides, my kids would never say, "The beginning is not being judged so I'm just going to kind of half do it." You want to leave the best impression that you can, and these kids would never pass up an opportunity to shine. They're competitors, they're fighters, and they're performers. They wouldn't even know how to go out there and half-do something in front of a crowd.

Finishing the routine that second time left the team exhausted but so happy. They knew they had nailed it. Backstage, everyone was hugging and bawling. Someone carried out Austin with his bandaged ankle so he could be a part of the circle. The team held hands and chanted: "I believe that together we will fly! I believe in the power of you and I!"

When it was time for the winner to be announced, Navarro took the stage next to Trinity Valley from Athens, Texas, as a girl in an NCA uniform brought out the second-place trophy. My team held one another and prayed as the announcer began: "In our junior college division, starting in second place, with a 97.2875, let's hear it for . . ."

The pause seemed to last for hours.

". . . Trinity Valley Community College!"

A look of gratitude and relief flooded my cheerleaders' faces. Some of them started to cry right then. And when their victory was announced, the team began jumping up and down, screaming, tears streaming down their faces.

"And the community college national champions, with a 97.8375, Navarro College!"

The feeling of victory was even sweeter for its having almost been taken away.

As tradition dictated, we all ran down to the beach, carrying the giant trophy and the NCA championship banner into the waves. Someone carried me into the surf, too, no matter that I was dressed in all my clothes. We all stood there together in the Florida sun, hair wet, covered in sand, smiling from ear to ear.

What the team learned that day was that all those rehearsals—*all* the getting it wrong, *all* the pushing through mistakes and problems—had made it inevitable that we'd succeed when it counted. People like to wish us luck when we head into competition, but it was clear to every one of us on that day at Daytona that luck had nothing to do with it. Our victory came from all those long hours in the gym—falling, running, doing push-ups, hitting play on the track for the thousandth time—failing as many times as it took so that when push came to shove, we couldn't help but get it right.

14

POINT. YOUR. TOES.
PERCEPTION IS REALITY

Y ou win a couple of times and people start to expect it. Every-where I go, people say, "You're gonna win this year, right?"

I say, "We're going to work our butts off and put in the hours. We're going to go do our very best." But *of course* I want to win. I don't want to disappoint anyone, and if the outcome is not in our favor, we're going to disappoint a lot of people. It's a heavy weight to carry.

I am reminded all the time that the team is our town's pride and joy. Our neighbors and classmates depend on us to work hard. They're invested in us winning—and in our setting a good example for others. When you're a coach in a close-knit community, you hear about every move your kids make. If anyone on the cheer team so much as looks at a can of beer or sasses an elder, my phone starts ringing.

Sometimes the level of scrutiny gets a little ridiculous. One man at a basketball game told me he wished the girls would smile more.

I tried to be polite as I said, "They've been in class and in practice and some of them had to go to work and then come straight to this game. They're a little tired, but sure, while they're doing stunts and keeping the audience's energy up for three hours, they'll try to smile, too."

Another time, someone told me they overheard a couple of my cheerleaders cussing at Walmart. The supposed ringleader was the most mild, soft-spoken girl on the team. I asked her about it and she blushed and said, "Well, I was just talking to my friend." Two girls are having what they think is a private conversation in the makeup aisle and suddenly I'm taking a break from my work to hear about it.

Then I have to go to my team and say, "For the duration of the season, can y'all just live in a bubble—don't curse, don't drink, don't do anything wrong—so I don't get these phone calls?"

For the most part they're good kids. They're probably your typical college kids, and the good thing is we're so busy that they don't have the downtime to get into too much trouble. A lot of them do All Star cheerleading on top of Navarro. If they're not here, they're usually at All Star cheer practice in Dallas. If they do have an off night, they're often at our gym, stunting.

In my twenty-six years, I have gotten a couple of emails from teachers telling me a student was disrespectful. That's something that will send me over the edge. I tell the student, "That's the one thing you can control. You can avoid being disrespectful to someone. I don't care how right you think you are. It does not matter. If you embarrass me, we're going to have a problem."

One thing I've noticed in my time with teenagers is that a lot of them don't realize or think about how they are being perceived or how they're affecting others. I find myself repeating: "How would you feel if somebody did blah blah blah to you?" It makes a difference when you start thinking about how you would feel on the receiving end, or even about how your actions affect your friends.

Usually the perception of a bad attitude or disrespect comes more from the way people speak to one another than what they are actually saying. I always say your body language is 80 percent of your communication. When it comes to teenagers, that means their slouching bodies are often sending the message, "I don't care what you're saying." One of the most important things cheerleaders learn over time is how to make what they're saying with their bodies line up with what's in their heads.

I once had a very talented male stunter on the team whose body language was terrible. He never said too much, but the way he carried himself and the way he would communicate through his sighs, shrugs, and eye rolls was like a cancer in the gym. The negative energy just flowed out of him from the moment he stepped into the room.

During my first conversation with him about this (yes, we had many!), he told me that he didn't know what I was talking about. He said that because he wasn't saying anything bad or ugly he thought he was being a team player. That is when I had to explain to him that his body language was coming through loud and clear, more so than his words. I shared with him something my former pastor once said: "If you're happy, you should notify your face." I think we made some progress throughout the year, but he still had a way to go when he was done at Navarro.

What I try to drill into the team from the very first practice is the awareness that no stunt will ever be perfect, and that perfection isn't as important as the *appearance* of perfection. If you're doing a hard stunt, it's very possible that sometimes you won't have a perfect grip. You won't have a perfect hold. How do you keep it from showing? Are you able to handle the bad grip? Are you always landing on your feet, no matter how badly the tumbling went? Are you able to keep the stunt in the air? It's amazing how far a pointed toe and a smile can go toward covering up an awkward position.

This is why I tell the team that a lot of the time, especially in competition, perception is reality. If it looks like you stuck your landing perfectly, you stuck your landing perfectly—even if in your heart of hearts you know that you were an inch off from where you should have been.

That means we have to work on our performance ability as much as we do on our skills. Two people can do the exact same move, and if one points her toes enthusiastically and smiles brightly, who's going to get the higher score?

This is also true in life. There are so many people who are sour at the world when they wake up. Why live like that? There's a domino effect. You wake up mad and everything's bound to make you mad—from the coffee not brewing fast enough to the traffic you're stuck in. Then the people you encounter are going to respond to your negativity and they're going to treat you in a way that perpetuates your bad mood. Faking it until you make it can have a wonderful effect on your day's outcome.

And why waste energy and time with the negative? I have my share of stress, but when I leave the house in the morning I'm ready to be happy. I'm hoping the day will be a good one. When I encounter a Bitter Betty, as I call the grumps, I think, *Geez. Do you want a cookie or a nap or something?*

You'd be amazed how many people think that being competitive means being nasty. Just because your team wins and mine didn't, I'm not going to be jealous or want you to fail. I've even seen some coaches sabotage other teams at their own schools, which you'd think would be beyond the pale. I'd still never talk trash about them.

Once our athletic director asked me point-blank about a coach we both know who was known to undermine other coaches whenever the chance arose.

"Oh gosh!" I said. "I mean . . . everyone's trying their best, and . . ." I flailed around for something nice to say. When I couldn't say anything nice I just stayed quiet.

"You can't ever say anything bad about *anybody*, can you?" he said.

Well, I *could*. But I won't. Because I need to lead by example. How would it look if I were to bad-mouth someone when I'm telling the kids every day, "Hey, guys, we can't be the best team we can be if y'all are fighting against each other instead of building each other up"? I also believe it all works out right in the end. Most of the people I've seen who tried to hurt others have ended up out of the business for one reason or another.

What's more, I want to live in harmony. Life is way more relaxing if you're trying to get along than if you wake up being miserable and looking for reasons to be mad. Maybe it's the Texan in me. Our state is super friendly. I always hear: "Let me hold the door open for you!" "How are you doing today?" Even if I'm in a bad mood, I can be friendly and engaging. I don't understand how people can't at least fake it. It's often true that while I'm pretending to be in a good mood, a good mood will take over and I'll forget why I was even grouchy in the first place.

If I'm ever having trouble rising to an occasion, I remember the first week they were filming *Cheer*, in January 2019. It was one of the hardest weeks of my life.

I went to a party on New Year's Eve, and in the next day or two I started running a fever and feeling really sick. Chris and I both got the flu. For three days, I couldn't move. I was asleep all day.

Before Christmas I'd received a call from the school asking me if the team could perform at a downtown pep rally on January 10. I freaked out, but made myself say: "Of course we can do it."

I knew that this would be a difficult task. The kids would have just gotten back into town and we would need to learn a routine that could be performed on a small stage.

The day after Christmas I had a meeting with our police chief, Chief Johnson, who was helping to coordinate the pep rally. I found out just how big a deal it was for the town. I always feel a lot of pressure when we have a performance, but this time seemed to carry a little more weight. A lot of important people would be there, including some who had never seen us in action. I didn't want to screw it up.

People in the community had been working hard to expand the downtown and bring more money into the town. And it had worked. Now on Saturdays, you can go shopping downtown and they serve mimosas in the stores. Corsicana was being considered for the TV show *Small Business Revolution*, in which experts revitalize a small town's business district. Ty Pennington and Amanda Brinkman visited our downtown. So the college and the business leaders wanted us to put our best foot forward at this pep rally.

Now it was the first week of January and I had the flu. I knew that I needed to recover fast, because I was about to be on a nonstop ride for the next few months. On that Sunday, the first day I was able to shower after fighting off my illness, I scrounged up enough energy to meet some of the kids at the gym to go over choreography and put together a routine for the pep rally. After a few hours we finalized everything and I went home and passed out.

Monday morning, I stepped away from my office for a moment when our marketing director called me on my cell.

"Hey, where you at?" she asked. I told her I was across the street making some copies but that I was on my way back.

She said, "The film crew's here for you to meet them."

I expected a small crew with a camera. Instead, there were at least fifteen of them. Fifteen!

That day, they filmed us practicing at the gym. Then I learned they wanted to come home with me to film us watching the Alabama football team compete for the national championship. Still weak from the flu, I hustled back home and cleaned my house. By the time the crew came over for the game, I thought it would be a miracle if they got any footage of me with my eyes open, but they seemed satisfied.

The following afternoon, I met with the committee overseeing the community support for the push to make it to the final selection for the TV show.

"Will you be a speaker?" one of the ladies asked me at the meeting.

"No, thank you," I said. "I'm getting over the flu. The truth is, I'm stressed out about filming this *Cheer* show plus coming up with choreography for the Corsicana pep rally. I don't want all that stress of having to speak as well."

The next day, we did our dress rehearsal at the venue. It went pretty well and I let the kids leave. I decided to stay and talk to Stacie Sipes, our marketing director, for a few minutes. I was sitting at the back of the auditorium and whispered to her, "They asked me to speak, but I was too stressed out about all this other stuff, and I told them no."

A moment later in the run-through of the speeches, I heard Navarro president Dr. Fegan say, "Monica's speaking next."

Stacie called out, "No! Remember? Monica's not talking."

He said, "If Monica wants to work here, she *is* talking."

"Oh!" I said. "Yes, you are correct. I *will* be speaking."

I turned to Stacie and said, "Well, I guess I should have snuck out of here when I had the chance!"

I walked up to the stage and grabbed the microphone. I thought, *I don't know what I'm going to say, but I'll do my best.* I proceeded to say that I had no idea what I would be speaking about but that I would definitely be ready when the time came.

It was a rough start to filming *Cheer*. But when you've got responsibilities, you've just got to get up and go. It doesn't matter if you're barely walking because you're getting over the flu. Now, post-COVID, this is (of course!) different.

Staying home when you're sick is now the best practice, as I learned when I came down with the coronavirus in January 2021. I got the vaccine on a Thursday. I woke up that Sunday nauseous and very weak. Thinking it was a side effect of the vaccine, I went to work Monday and wound up, just hours later, lying on the floor of my office because I couldn't sit up and was sick to my stomach. I felt like I was shaking from the inside out. I was trying to tell Andy something and I couldn't even think of the simple words. One of my girls tested positive, so I got tested and found out it wasn't the vaccine—I'd caught COVID. For days I was weak, congested, nauseous, and could barely move.

Coronavirus aside, as long as you're not contagious and not endangering anyone else, I think it's usually in your best interest to push through personal discomfort and keep going. And thank God I didn't just stay in bed that week in 2019! If I had let the stress get to me and bailed out of the rally or the show, who knows? All the amazing things that have happened this year might not have happened and you might not be reading this book right now.

Rising to meet the occasion—keeping those toes pointed and that smile big, no matter what's going wrong—is what gives you the best possible chance of success.

15

FIND INSPIRATION
EVERYWHERE

Seeking out things that motivate you—each and every day— helps build excellence into whatever you set out to do. Whether you are looking for a spark of creativity or to maintain energy for a long-term project, there are possibilities all around you. It may be a certain song that gets you pumped or a quiet moment in nature that gives you focus or an inspirational Instagram account that keeps you positive. When you keep yourself open to things that might influence you for the better, you start to find them everywhere.

About thirteen years ago, I was sitting on the couch watching *Dancing with the Stars*. Suddenly I grabbed Chris's arm. "Look at that!" I shouted. I scribbled some figures in a notebook I have with me at all times so I can jot down ideas as they occur to me.

"What?" he said. He saw an intricate dance routine on-screen but nothing more.

When the man swung his female partner around his head I'd seen a vision of our next pyramid.

We would have a guy in what's called a prep—on top of two other guys holding his feet so he's standing on their hands. Close by, there would be two guys holding a girl close to the ground, about to throw her. The guy in the air would take her hand and then the others would toss her so she swung around his head, her body straight out, with her legs in a V shape, as though she were doing an ice-skating move. She would swing around his head and then come back into the structure, ending up on top of everyone else at the top of the pyramid. It would be so pretty.

The next day in practice I gathered the team around me and said, "I have an idea!"

Groans. Faces hidden in hands. Fear.

"What's the problem?" I asked.

"Anytime you say you have an idea, we wind up doing something bizarre," one of the cheerleaders said.

I described what I'd seen on TV to the team. "And then you flip her around like *this*!" I waved my hand in the air to demonstrate.

They looked at me in horror. I heard one tell another that they should confiscate my remote to save them from any more "inspiration." They told me they'd like to monitor my viewing from now on, to keep me from seeing anything else too athletic.

The kids still give me a hard time because once I was watching *The Biggest Loser* and saw that they made everybody who was competing run a mile within a certain time limit. Some of them couldn't do it. As I was watching the show I thought, *Surely everybody on my team could do that.* So I came to practice the next day and I said, "Okay, so I was watching *The Biggest Loser* last night, and I know y'all can do this. But to be safe I need you to show me. I'm going to time y'all. Run a mile."

They thought I was joking at first, but I wasn't. I started my stopwatch and they took off. They could all do it, it turned out, but they certainly did not like it. And team veterans still bring it up to me now, years later: "Remember when you watched that dang show *The Biggest Loser*, and you made us run a mile?"

But I don't apologize for it. I felt like I had to make sure they could meet that baseline level of fitness. When I saw they could do it, I was satisfied.

Outside of the cheer world, one person who inspires me the most is Taylor Swift. She is just plain brilliant at her job, the complete package. Her songwriting is incredible. I'm amazed by how easily she moves back and forth between genres, from pop to country, perfect at both. I've seen her in concert every time she's come through Texas. What an incredible performer and storyteller, not to mention what a good role model for girls! She doesn't care what people think of her. She does Taylor. She knows she's a good person and has the guts to do what she does best without regard for the people who want to bring her down. The word for her is also the title of one of her albums: *Fearless*. During tough times, when I need to be fearless, I listen to her music and she gives me strength.

In one of the interviews I did during the *Cheer* press tour in 2020, I mentioned that Taylor Swift was one of my favorite celebrities and that I had her songs on all my playlists.

Amazingly, within days of that interview, an email arrived from someone claiming to be her publicist. My first thought was that it had to be a joke. The email said that Taylor wanted to send me a gift. I googled the emailer's name and learned that she was legit: Tree Paine had even appeared in the Taylor Swift documentary *Miss Americana*.

After I confirmed the email from Taylor's publicist wasn't a prank, I emailed her back and said, "You've made my year. Please tell Taylor that we're huge fans. We've been to every concert when she's come through Dallas. My daughter sang 'Mean' in her fifth-grade talent show."

She wrote back: "Thank you. I'll make sure and tell Taylor. You'll make her day."

Two days later, Taylor announced that she was dropping a new album, *Folklore*. I got it and immediately started listening to it non-stop on repeat. One of my favorite songs on the album was "Cardigan."

The same day her album dropped, a box arrived. There was a note reading, "I hope this cardigan will keep you warm and cozy in these extremely un-cozy times. Sending you a socially distanced hug and all my love, Taylor." Inside a tissue-paper wrapping was a cardigan sweater with a few stars on the sleeve and Taylor's name on it. So now we're best friends. (I don't know if Taylor knows it yet, but we are.)

Our sources of inspiration do not always give us sweaters, but whatever form they take, they leave us invigorated and open us up to new possibilities. The 2007 routine that came to be known as our *Dancing with the Stars* pyramid won for us in Daytona. It looked terrifying, but it wasn't actually that dangerous. My vision worked out. And even the most skeptical members of the team had to admit it was fun.

My kids always think I'm a little eccentric when it comes to pyramids, because I always have outrageous ideas. Most of the time, they don't work out. But that's not for lack of trying.

Looking for new ideas everywhere fosters creativity and keeps you open to learning every day. There's no area of life in which that openness to experience and inspiration isn't helpful, whether it's trying to think up innovations at work, fun things to do with your family, or adventures to go on with your friends.

My habit of finding inspiration everywhere has become almost a joke by this point. The kids will tag me on an Instagram video of circus acts with the caption "Don't let Monica see this."

16

RECRUIT THE
RIGHT TEAMMATES

I n my early days at Navarro, I knew I needed a mentor to help me find my footing, and I was lucky enough to find one in a former coach of mine: Louis Huston. Louis grew up in a rough part of the South Bronx and then wound up a successful businessman in Texas with horses and a ranch. (He likes to compare himself to Billy Crystal in *City Slickers*.)

Before his work in the corporate world, he'd been on the cheerleading judging circuit for many years and did a little freelance choreography. He had choreographed Jeri and me in our high school's varsity routine for nationals. (He put me toward the back of the pyramid because he thought I seemed shy.) My first full year of coaching, I reached out to him to ask if he'd work with Navarro.

He choreographed for us for a couple of years, and even though he's reluctant to take credit, he, more than anyone else, helped me put together the blueprint for Navarro's program.

The first thing he said to me was, "Take care of the kids like they're yours. Cheerleading is cheerleading. What you're coaching these kids on is life. You've got to make these kids know that this is *their* goal, not your goal." Louis explained that once I gave them the tools, it would be up to them to execute. But it was my job to stay on top of them. "You're the mama bear," he said. "You make them pay when they need to. You reward them when you need to. And you've got to be soft when you need to."

The other advice he gave me was to always prepare ahead. In those first years we were going to Daytona, Louis and I would go out to lunch the day after the competition and talk through what had gone well and gone poorly. Louis was strategic. He would say, "Okay, given all that, what do you need to do for next year? What skills do you need? What skills beat you or what skills do you want to improve upon? What pyramids did you enjoy? What tumbling passes?"

Even after Louis retired to pursue a number of different projects, he's remained my number one mentor. I know that I can call him anytime for anything—and I do. It was him I turned to when the *Cheer* producers called and wanted to do a show. He said it was a no-brainer, because it was a once-in-a-lifetime opportunity and I clearly trusted the production crew of *Cheer*. They were sincere and hardworking, and if I ever hoped to help spread the message about how serious a sport cheerleading is, I would need people on my team like them.

When the crew came to film the team in early 2019, the director, Greg, said they were going to try to pick a few kids to focus on.

He said no matter who they chose they knew they'd get great stories but that they wanted to show a real diversity of experience.

I gave Greg and his team a few names of cheerleaders whose stories I found especially moving and they spent a couple of days talking to them. I thought it was interesting that when Greg and his crew watched us practice and then met up to talk about which kids they wanted to follow, they all had the same list: Morgan, La'Darius, Jerry Harris, Lexi, Gabi, and actually many others. They said it was difficult to narrow it down. Everyone had a story, so it really could have been any of the kids.

Gabi Butler is one of the stars of the cheer community, and she has countless young fans thanks to her popular YouTube channel. Some viewers have told me that they felt that Gabi's parents came across on the show as overbearing. But I guarantee you that their investment is not uncommon when it comes to top-tier athletes! I can also tell you that they are truly great people. I was surprised at some of the backlash. The thing is, they don't pretend to be anyone but themselves: the very first scene they're in features them on the couch arguing over who was going to be the one to tell a particular story. Most people would go out of their way to put on a show for the cameras, but not the Butlers. What you see is what you get.

Their home is open to kids in need in a way that exemplifies human kindness. If a cheerleader winds up in a tough spot and needs a place to sleep for a night or for a month, they go to the Butlers' house. That family would give you the shirts off their backs. And they have made sacrifices in order to give Gabi opportunities that she otherwise would not have had. The Butlers know that supporting an athlete in the upper echelon of a sport requires the whole family's investment in terms of money, time, and enthusiasm.

Even as Greg and the crew filmed Gabi and her family, as well as the others they had selected to follow, they kept feeling tempted to add in even more athletes' stories. But ultimately, even though the whole team was interesting, they knew it was best to stick with fewer subjects. They wanted to go deep with each main character rather than just getting little bits of information from a lot of people.

Obviously, their priority was getting intimate stories. At first I was alarmed by how much time they were planning to spend looking into these kids' lives, going into their dorms and even visiting their homes. I felt protective of the kids, and I lost sleep trying to balance the potential upside to their having this opportunity with what could amount to a loss of their privacy.

But as time went on, I got to know the people involved in the show very well. As it turned out, everyone Greg hired was sensitive and considerate. He found smart and compassionate crew members, mostly women. I've heard them talk about the show since then and they all say the same thing: *We became a family.* I was able to grow confident that they would do right by my kids.

One of the producers on the show, Chelsea Yarnell, always wanted to shoot everything, everywhere. She's a great person with a hippie vibe—tall and thin with short, curly hair and glasses. She can talk me into just about anything (which I've learned is one sign of a great producer).

In one interview, Chelsea said, "We just lucked out with these characters. Any filmmaker will tell you: access is everything. They were so generous. They let us into their lives."

Associate producer Cinnamon Triano said the best part was that the production team's location near the gym meant that the kids would pass by them on the way in and give them hugs. They said that the show revealed how beautifully a genuinely diverse group of people—rich and poor, black and white, straight and gay—can work to support one another.

When the crew first came to the gym, I think we scared them to death. They weren't used to seeing people flying through the air or falling into outstretched arms. It took the camera team a couple of days, maybe even more, to get used to what we were doing, so they wouldn't gasp out loud when someone did a hard tumbling pass. The producers wanted to get great shots, so the cameras got close. Once or twice, they got too near and a body flew terrifyingly close to a lens.

Greg was always afraid a camera would get in the way of a cheerleader, resulting in an accident, but his cinematographers, Erynn Patrick and Melissa Langer, were total pros. They seemed to always know the exact second to run for cover. They were shooting with prime lenses, which meant they couldn't zoom in. They just had to get used to what we were doing in our routine, to know their comfort zone and how close they could get. They almost became part of the team's choreography.

I have so many fond memories of that crew. One afternoon when we were practicing for a pep rally, the crew members went down the line and introduced themselves, and when the team learned Cinnamon's name they lost it. Cheerleaders are always welcoming. But if something strikes them as particularly delightful, they will turn it up to the next level. When Cinnamon said her name, everyone on the team started jumping around, shouting, "Heyyyyyy, *Cinnnnnammmmonnnn!*"

For fun one afternoon we convinced Erynn—a dead ringer for Allie—to put on a Navarro uniform. She looked just like one of the girls on the team. We laughed so hard that day.

My favorite times were when the crew brought in specialty equipment and we got to learn how it worked. Once, they showed up with a Segway, put a camera on it, and kept zipping in and out of the middle of the gym on it. We thought it was the coolest thing ever, especially when the cameraman filmed Lexi tumbling by, following her whole routine as he moved right along with her on that thing. At one point, Lexi got a little too close to him while tumbling and we all tensed up, but they didn't collide. And it was worth it. The video from the Segway was incredible to watch. When I think back on that day now, I remember the fear that they'd crash and the relief that they didn't.

After the filming was over, I got the sweetest messages from people on the crew. They talked about how we inspired them and how sad it was that we would no longer see one another every day.

Still, even with the trust that had grown between us, watching the show was a real moment of truth. I was so nervous. It was a big risk. I had no idea what they were going to do with the footage. In TV, they can edit those hundreds of hours in such a way that it might be all about drama, or they could have twisted things I said. You have to trust who's doing the work. And I did. From the moment that I met Greg, I trusted that he simply wanted to tell a true story.

That said, I was terrified to see the show. *What if I was wrong to put so much faith in Greg and his crew? What if I was wrong to say yes to this project?* I wondered endlessly about what they kept and what they cut. As I opened the link to the show I thought, *Here's the moment of truth.*

Chris, Ally, Austin, and I gathered around the TV and I pushed play timidly.

"Why are you so nervous?" Chris asked me. "You were there for the shooting. You know what's going to be on the show."

I tried to tell him that I didn't know, really, but I just settled in and let the show wash over me. We sat there riveted for six hours straight. We started watching in the late afternoon and it was 11 p.m. before we turned off the TV.

It was a six-hour roller coaster of emotion. During the final episode, when we were in Daytona, I was shaking. I felt anxious. I felt sick. I felt, in short, exactly like I do when I'm in Daytona.

In the course of those six hours, I laughed. I cried. All the emotions came up. The show held up a mirror to the team. We were able to see more clearly than ever how much the sport meant to us and how exciting it all was.

When the six hours of the show was over, I turned off the TV, feeling pride and profound relief: *Okay, I don't think I'm going to get fired for anything on there.* I felt like Greg and the crew had taken all that raw material and told a true story, a beautiful story. I was so glad I'd trusted my instincts and trusted them with our lives.

Over the next couple of months during the press events for the show, I noticed the cheerleaders seemed happy and comfortable. Even sitting on Ellen's couch, they weren't rattled. Our producer Chelsea said that the long hours and hard work we did in practice paid off: "If you can get through the stress of Daytona, you can get through anything."

Obviously, there were some things I got nailed for in the media afterward. Most everything was positive, but some people took issue with various things, as people will. The main thing was the number of times we were shown falling from a stunt or pyramid. They equated falls with injuries, which is far from the truth. We actually don't have a lot of injuries during the year. We have your typical wear and tear that needs rehabbing but not a lot of significant injuries. Mackenzie "Sherbs" Sherburn's fall, which caused a dislocated elbow, was a fluke that just happened to be shown to the whole world.

I tried to explain that this was an edited TV show. They showed every single time we fell over several months, and not all the thousands of times we did the same thing and hit it perfectly. For the record, in my twenty-six years of coaching, we've had very few broken bones.

Chris told me I shouldn't read the negative comments. I teach my kids that mental health is important, and so I had to practice what I preach. I thought, *Why read something that's only going to bring me down?* People who watched the show saw only saw six hours of footage shot over months. Chris said no one could really know me based just on that.

I am thankful for those people who keep me grounded, tell me when I screw up, celebrate me when I succeed, and have my back no matter what. I invited Louis to come down to Corsicana one day when I knew the *Cheer* crew would be there filming. I'd talked about him so much that the crew was eager to interview him. But I didn't tell him they'd be there, because I knew he'd be too humble to show up if he knew.

He walked into the gym, saw the crew, and as he was hugging me, he whispered, "Uh, do you have a microphone on your body right now?"

"Yes," I said.

"I am going to kill you," he said.

"I knew you wouldn't come if I told you!" I said. "They want to talk to you and they want you on the show."

Louis just said, "Oh no. This is not how we roll." And then he found a spot out of the camera's line of sight. But you can't hide from the printed page, Louis! You are my hero, my security blanket, and my friend—and no matter what is going on, I will always want you on my team.

17

WE CAN! WE WILL! WE MUST...
PREPARE FOR SURPRISES

When we lost in 2017 because of those two little unforeseeable mistakes, I vowed to do everything in my power to keep such things from happening again. Both of the errors, it occurred to me, were caused by our team's lack of familiarity with the conditions in Daytona.

We're used to practicing in the gym on what we call a "dead floor" or a "hard floor." Basically, our floor is just made of mats rolled out onto the wooden gym floor. Sometimes we'll go outside and roll the mats out on the concrete. We do that because at competition we do prelims inside an arena on mats rolled out onto the concrete floor. And at finals, you go outside and you're next to the beach on the stage. So you have the sunlight hitting you and sometimes a lot of wind.

That Daytona stage is different from anything back home for a few reasons even beyond the sun and the wind. For one thing, the floor is a little bit bouncy. The wooden panels have a little bit of give. So when you're tumbling and you have all this adrenaline, you're *used* to punching really hard to land on your feet on that dead floor and then suddenly you've got your adrenaline amped up and a little bit of bounce, and you have to control how you land so you don't over-rotate. In 2017, one of the mistakes happened because a girl did just that. She probably had too much adrenaline and then that extra little bounce caused her over-rotation. The stage in Daytona is also, of course, elevated. The other error that year came when a girl felt like the mat was shorter than what we'd normally practiced on.

The day after we lost the finals in 2017, I was talking to the parents of one of my cheerleaders, Danielle Fleming, and I said, "We were prepared. The only thing we could've done different would have been to have a stage to practice on. . . ." And the light bulb went on. "What we need to do is build a stage," I said. As luck would have it, Danielle's dad was in the construction business and said he thought he could build us a stage.

I took a little delegation to the Daytona venue and talked to the people who'd built the stage there. We took pictures of it underneath so we could see how it was constructed. And Danielle's dad drew out a whole sketch and figured out what materials we would need and how much it would cost for us to build it.

It was going to be expensive. We're used to fundraising to help pay for some of our expenses in Daytona above and beyond what's in our school budget—it's a pricey trip. We have to fly dozens of people there, get a hotel, pay the registration fees. We organize an annual fundraiser where the kids solicit sponsorships for the backs of the shirts we wear to Daytona, whether it's a local business or a family member buying a line: "Good luck! Love, Grandma."

In 2019, the school got a bit of money from Netflix that we were able to put into our fundraising account. Then we got $20,000 from *Ellen*. If I was ever going to get my stage, it seemed like this was the year to go for it.

I talked to someone over at buildings and maintenance. He said, "Well, if we're going to have this structure, it has to have an actual set of blueprints that are approved. We want to make sure that it's built sound and with the stamp of an engineer."

It was decided that since we only need the stage for a few weeks every year we'd erect it in the parking lot in the weeks leading up to Daytona and then we'd take it apart and store it for the rest of the year. So we had to buy two shipping containers to keep it in. We painted the containers green to match the neighboring John Deere program.

For me, this stage is the final piece of the puzzle for how to fully prepare. I want to make sure we've gone through every scenario we possibly can, anticipated every obstacle, and ritualized our reaction to each step and bounce and ray of sunshine we possibly can.

When I first started asking around about building a stage, I heard from everyone: "Oh, well, that's going to be a little bit difficult."

I said, "I'm fine with difficult."

★

Every aspect of cheerleading involves unexpected twists: how people perform, how the team changes in the course of the season, even how we get from place to place. Of course, this is true of all aspects of life. Uncertainty is a big part of being human. No matter how hard we work or how much we try to do the right thing, we may struggle to find our place in the world or a nourishing romantic relationship or a career we love. All we have complete control over is our own attitude.

At one competition, during a preliminary round, we were given a deduction for having "an illegal pyramid." Louis and I were there together and we both became enraged by that ruling. Our pyramid was not illegal. Louis was ready to run over to the judge and start yelling at him but I talked him off the ledge. This was just preliminary. We decided to put our heads together and figure out what the judge thought he had seen; then we could prove him wrong in the actual competition. Once we thought we knew, we told the cheerleader who'd made the supposedly false move to hit the right way very demonstratively during the routine and then look directly at the judge. It worked. And in that moment, we also realized that we could use the feedback we got in prelims to make changes that would guarantee higher scores in the finals.

Being prepared for surprises may not always be possible. One of the first times the crew came to film us for *Cheer* was for a ceremony at which we handed out the 2018 national championship rings to the team members. The ceremony took place at the Corsicana Country Club before a homecoming football game. There was a buffet set out and a lot of pomp as we received our rings for that year's Daytona win.

In years past, by the time the rings arrived everyone was back home for the summer, so we just mailed the rings to everyone's homes. But that year I wanted to start doing something special. Nearly everyone on the team was able to attend. We showed a little highlight video and reminisced about all that we'd been through together. It was such a moving day. Toward the end, the weather turned. People's phones began chirping with alerts—a tornado warning.

In Texas, we're used to tornado warnings. We'll get an alert and say, "Oh, a tornado? Let me walk outside and see!" Yes, I know— probably not the smartest thing to do.

Well, the film crew's not from Texas. They're from Los Angeles and New York. They hear "tornado" and they start totally freaking out. One of them came up to me, white as a sheet, and said, "Okay, we're scared. But, judging by how all of you guys are acting, maybe we shouldn't be? We're not used to this. But if you all aren't freaking out, then we're going to assume we shouldn't freak out?"

I looked at the weather tracker on my phone and said, "Oh, this tornado is twenty miles away from us! We're fine."

I could see on their faces that they were still concerned. But I wasn't worried. So they just kept filming.

When the ceremony ended I said, "I'm going to run home and change into my rain boots before the game starts. I'll see y'all at the game. Why don't you hang out here and finish off the buffet?"

Well, while I was at home changing shoes, the tornado went right by the football field. The wind picked up, gusting to seventy miles per hour. Torrential rain—then hail—pounded the bleachers. Branches and debris littered the ground.

Oops. Sometimes my weather predictions miss the mark. The film crew had to take shelter in the hallway at the country club. The campus police told me to stay home until further notice. The kids who were still back at the dorms sought refuge in their bathtubs and the ones who were already at the football field were ushered into the nearby middle school for protection.

An hour or two later, we got the all-clear and I drove out to the game, which had been delayed. The band had bailed. I asked for the school sound system to be brought to the field so we could play the fight song over the loudspeakers and wouldn't have to cheer in silence. In spite of everything, our team played one of the best games ever. The game went into overtime, and we ended up winning. So even if nature doesn't cooperate, you can make the best of things. When it was all over, I went up to the crew and said, "Well, I think we got y'all some pretty good footage today: ring ceremony, tornado, overtime game, victory. Let's see what we can arrange for tomorrow!"

They laughed, but they also looked a little nervous.

The truth is, we had no idea what to expect when the Netflix crew started following us around a couple of years ago. It seemed like forever from when we started talking about it, to the first time they filmed, to when the series was actually finished. You're putting yourself at risk if you're going to be on a TV show, because you don't know how it's going to be edited. You have no idea how they're going to portray you.

When filming first started in January 2019, we were very conscious of the cameras, but by a week in we'd totally forgotten they were there. I was so surprised when the show aired in 2020 because it not only accomplished what I wanted—showing how athletic and serious cheerleading is—but it also portrayed the kids' stories in such a sensitive, beautiful way.

The day *Cheer* came out, January 8, people started talking about it immediately. It came out at two in the morning our time. And all of my kids—of course—stayed up all night watching it into the wee hours of the morning.

Throughout the next day, people started to post about it. They had to have binge-watched it for six hours straight, as I had!

As I was going about my day, I kept getting messages—first in a trickle, then in a flood: "I never thought I would watch a docuseries about cheerleading; I loved it!" "What a joyful show!" "I'm so inspired!"

Of course some people sent me awful messages: "Go to hell!" "You're torturing these kids!" "Bitch!"

That's always going to happen if you're in the public eye. Luckily, I was accustomed to being criticized as a coach, and that experience had prepared me for this. When you lose, everyone wants to tell you why. When you win, everyone wants to tear you down. This was simply that phenomenon on a much larger scale. But I was happy to see that most of the people weighing in on my social media pages were incredibly positive.

A few days after the show aired, we went on *The Kidd Kraddick Morning Show*, a syndicated multi-host radio show that tapes in Dallas. I felt like we'd hit the big time. I'm a huge *Kidd Kraddick* fan. I've been listening to that show since it debuted in the early '90s (which is when some of the newer hosts on the show were born).

Two days later, I got a call that said, "Ellen wants you to come on the show next week." *The Ellen DeGeneres Show* wanted to interview us *and* have the team perform on their stage—in less than a week.

So we went from zero to a hundred really fast. We weren't prepared for any of it. Several of the cheerleaders were in other states. That Friday we mapped out a plan that we could put into action on Monday, when we had everyone together.

Monday was crazy! We had a recruit clinic that had been scheduled for months, so we had to work our practices around that. We did an early morning practice and then hosted the recruit clinic from 1 p.m. until 3 p.m. After a break for dinner we were back in the gym running through the routine that we would be performing on national television just two days later. Somehow in the craziness of the day's events, I lost my car keys and had to have my car towed so I could get a new set made.

I was completely worn out by the time I got home that night. As I was packing at around 11 p.m., I got a call saying that Spotify had invited us to attend their pre–Grammy Awards party. Now things were getting really weird. The *Grammys*? I stared at my closet. I had nothing red-carpet ready. The best I could do was pants, a jacket, and some sparkly heels. I threw them in with the jeans and shirts I'd packed.

The next day, Tuesday morning, I had everyone come in for one last practice before we headed to the airport. Then we all flew to L.A. On Wednesday, we arrived at the Warner Bros. Studio in Burbank, where they film *The Ellen DeGeneres Show*. Everything was moving so fast. Suddenly someone came up and brushed my hair and someone else powdered my face and then the door opened and I was out onstage in front of a studio audience. It was bizarre how sped-up everything felt that day. It was not enjoyable in the sense of, "Wow, this is fun!" because I was terrified. What if I tripped on my way to the couch? What if the kids all got hurt on the mat we had to work with, which was far smaller than regulation? I had to stop and give myself some mat talk to get in the right headspace.

And luckily, it all went great!

That night we had dinner at the Netflix building. The food was delicious and everyone was in the highest spirits; the *Ellen* appearance had been a triumph. Most of the team flew home the next morning, but some of us stayed in Los Angeles to do more interviews.

On Thursday, we did media all day. They took us from one appearance to the next, from a podcast to a newspaper interview to a social media stunt. Publicists and show handlers kept handing me scripts for segments. "I'm a coach, not an actress!" I said, but they just told me to memorize the lines, and I did my best.

Our schedule was so packed that I didn't have time to eat. It was exhausting. I'd never had a Red Bull in my life, but I drank three that day. Chris was out and about on his own. I called him and said, "I don't know where you're at, but I don't care if you have to bring me a loaf of bread. I need something to eat or I'm going to pass out." He showed up with a croissant from Dunkin' Donuts and fed me while I got dressed for the pre-Grammys party. It tasted like heaven.

At the party, we were feet away from Lizzo as she was performing her hits. She came out with so much energy and danced her butt off with her incredible backup dancers. We practically shouted along to "Truth Hurts" and "Good as Hell."

All the other people nominated for Best New Artist performed that night, including Billie Eilish, Lil Nas X, and Maggie Rogers. It was amazing to me how far our little community college cheer team had come in just a few days. The next morning we were back up early, doing spots on *Entertainment Tonight*, *Access Hollywood*, and *E! News*.

My mom called and said, "I saw you on *Access Hollywood*."

"Cool!" I said. "It was one of a dozen things we shot yesterday. This has been the wildest trip."

"On the show you looked kind of tired," she said.

I told her she didn't have to fill me in on that one.

★

If my life in cheer hadn't prepared me to be surprised at every turn, I don't think I would have survived it. The experience validated my belief that being prepared yet also flexible enough to roll with the punches is key to nailing a cheer routine and also to surviving whatever life throws at us—even national attention.

That year had been completely surreal from start to finish. The insanity reached a peak in the *Saturday Night Live* skit about us, which made fun of all the falls on the show. Some people in the cheer world were offended, but I told people who didn't like the skit, "No, that's what *SNL* is for. It's a parody. You're supposed to be made fun of. That means you've made it. We've made it!"

Chris and I laughed so hard watching that skit. In that moment, it was clear to us that cheerleading was now ready for both prime time and not–prime time, and I couldn't have been prouder.

18

MAKE THE BEST
OF A BAD SITUATION

I don't think anyone was prepared for 2020. Over the course of the year, our plans (like those of most people across the country) had to change day by day. It goes against my entire being: I like to know what's happening a year out. My beloved planner saw so many things crossed out. I had to learn a new skill: to relax and not let the uncertainty bother me too much.

Just three months after the show debuted, COVID-19 shut down our school and all that went with it. We were still planning to return that summer for camp, with safety protocols in place. Everybody was going to have to get tested for the virus. If anybody tested positive, anyone they were around would have to quarantine. I thought that might be tough to enforce, because a lot of the kids take each other to the grocery store or pick each other up at the airport. When they're so dependent on one another it's kind of impossible to say, "Get to Corsicana, but don't be around anyone until you get a test and receive a negative result."

I have so many kids from out of state—and I'm responsible for all of them. I had no idea how it would work if someone tested positive. I was full of questions: *Should I have them tested before leaving home, and then tested again when they get here? Should they quarantine in their dorm rooms before our first practice? Should they wear masks during practice?* My mind was spinning with possible scenarios. Finally, in June, I got on the phone with Andy for quite a while to make a plan for heading to camp that summer for the usual few intense days.

I told Andy, "Well, let's just take a smaller group, and that way we can control it better, and we'll just start with who feels comfortable traveling during this pandemic and go from there." He agreed.

I typed up a long message on our group chat and explained the situation.

As soon as I sent this message, people started texting me and saying, "I want to come! I want to be a part of it!"

Then, ten minutes later, I got an email saying camp had been canceled. So after all this time trying to plan, the decision was made for us.

Camp getting canceled was a relief, because I'd been stressing out about how to handle it if someone tested positive. At the end of June, we'd just brought our football team in for summer practice. One player tested positive, so his roommates and suitemates had to go into quarantine. Then our assistant athletic trainer developed symptoms. Everybody entered quarantine until the tests came back—fortunately, they were negative. But it was a wake-up call. Our athletic department had to learn a lot, and fast.

Then in July of 2020 we heard that all fall sports would be moved to the spring. That completely turned around how our year would look. Our fall semester is usually so busy. Every afternoon in a typical fall week is normally spent cheering for volleyball and soccer in addition to practicing. On Tuesdays and Thursdays we do two-a-days, meaning we have practice at night in addition to our day-time practice. So a cheerleader's schedule might be Monday night volleyball game, Tuesday night practice, Wednesday soccer, Thursday night practice, Friday volleyball tournament, Saturday football game. How would we combine all that with what we already do in the spring? Well, we'd get through it if we had to. I'd been whipped last year by the time Christmas break came around, because we were involved in so many things. We typically do a lot of community service on top of our practices. That was all canceled, too.

Facing such unexpected challenges, I realized I had to try to look for silver linings and to focus on what *was* rather than what was not. One thing I found to be grateful for was that in the past I'd almost never gotten to go to see my daughter cheer at SMU football games because I'm always with Navarro teams on those days. But the SMU football games weren't canceled during 2020—so I could now show up for my daughter in a way I never had before. It didn't change that it would be tough having such a different fall semester, but the opportunity to show up for Ally was positive. I could find comfort there.

★

When I reached out to the cheerleaders to give them the news about the fall, I knew they'd also need help in processing the disappointment. Some of them would need more information and more support, and so I made sure to ask them more than once if they were okay or if they wanted to talk through the plan in more detail.

And to all of them, I emphasized we'd have to work hard to figure out how to turn this into something positive. Usually in the fall, we might get tired of cheering every day, but we love it. We might complain sometimes about spending hours and hours out in the sun or the rain every single Saturday, but those are actually the times when we wind up making some of the best memories.

I told them they'd need to get rest and begin preparing for an unprecedented spring, cheering for every single sport, all while preparing for Daytona. In the long run, it would offer us a brand-new kind of opportunity to prove ourselves.

And of course, the film crew had been there to cover all of this craziness, too. The week back in March when everything fell apart because of COVID, it was spring break and we had been practicing our Daytona routine nonstop for weeks. The routine looked amazing, and everybody was feeling good and ready for nationals, which were to take place in early April. We had our plane tickets. We believed we could have gone to compete right that minute if we needed to, because we were feeling that good. That was a Wednesday. Going into a long weekend, Andy and I sent the cheerleaders off to enjoy what remained of their spring break: "Goodbye. Get a few days off. Rest your bodies. We'll be back Monday, ready to go!"

That next day, Thursday, March 12, the NBA announced it was suspending its season. Soon everything else fell like dominoes.

Chelsea, one of the producers, called me and asked, "What are you doing? Where are you?"

I said, "I have a hair appointment."

"We have to come film that!" she said.

"No, Chelsea," I said, "you're not going to come film my hair appointment." Because, you know, I don't need the world to see me with dye all over my head.

But Chelsea is not one to be dissuaded.

"Monica, please, we have to film that!" she said.

Then I heard myself say, "Fine, okay, Chelsea. Meet me at Tangles."

She always has a way of getting to me. Then I called Andy and I said, "Where are you? We need to talk."

He was in Dallas and said, "I'm going to come back right now."

I said, "Fine. Come up to Tangles, where I'm getting my hair done." Everyone would be there. Why not make it a party?

Andy ran in, ignored the film crew documenting my hair all in foils, and shouted, "What are we going to do about the season?"

While still at Tangles, Andy and I called someone from the National Cheerleaders Association to ask them what the plan was. It was not the most relaxed salon day I've ever had, but Chelsea was happy.

"You know we're going to use all of this," she said as we left the salon, me with my new highlights and traces of hair dye lingering along my hairline.

I said, "Chelsea, I really didn't need you to film me with my hair crazy."

She just smiled and said, "Now what are y'all doing?"

We were hungry, so they came and filmed us talking while we ate.

19

THE JOY OF WORK

There is something about work that I love. It's not the crazy hours, the time away from my family, the stress of competing, or the anxiety of watching over college kids. It's the teamwork, the goal-setting, the little moments of success that build to bigger accomplishments. It's watching kids grow to become successful adults who have carried with them things I have said and lessons I've taught them. There is no better feeling than watching young adults blossom and thrive right in front of your eyes.

I have always loved working. I love the structure, the sense of purpose. As soon as I was able to drive, I got a job at Catfish King. I had to wear a red collared shirt and a cap with a furry ball on the top. Sometimes I would work the drive-through, which was my favorite. I would make up chants and welcome people with a cheer. It was fun, and I loved making the customers smile.

I was so good at my job that I would sometimes get tips in a restaurant where you ordered from the counter. I didn't need the money—my parents gave me a weekly allowance—but I loved working for my own paycheck and the feeling of having responsibilities.

This was while I was a varsity cheerleader in high school. We had cheer practice after school, so I would go straight to work from practice. I would close the store at night and get home around 10 p.m. to start on my homework. I was in advanced classes and took school very seriously. I never skipped out on my studies.

I worked several jobs throughout my high school and college years: lifeguard, sales associate at Bealls department store, intern at the Austin Chamber of Commerce.

For a while in Austin, I worked as a receptionist at Rick's Hair Salon on Guadalupe Street. Guadalupe was the center of campus life and commonly known only as the Drag. I answered phones, cleaned the tanning beds, and kept the shop tidy. The owner, Rick, looked more like a motorcycle gang member than a hairstylist, but he had a heart of gold and I loved working for him.

Fun fact: the movie *Dazed and Confused* was being filmed in Austin during this time and some of the cast came in to get their nails done. I had no idea at the time that I was one degree separated from the then-unknown Matthew McConaughey.

I graduated from college a semester early, so I was only twenty-one when I got my first *real* job. Chris and I had settled down near Dallas—Las Colinas, to be exact. I worked at a computer company for a year before getting the job at Navarro College and moving back to Corsicana.

We decided to start a family about a year after I began coaching. I was on a ten-month contract, which meant I had a few weeks off in the summer. I wanted to be strategic when planning the pregnancy and not have to miss any work, so we tried for a May baby. Our plan worked perfectly. We had our first child, Austin, in May 1996. The timing could not have been better. We had our graduation ceremony at Navarro on May 11 and I had Austin on the sixteenth. I made it through the semester and through the graduation ceremony before becoming a mother.

When Chris and I decided to have our second child, we were hoping to have a girl, but of course would have been happy with any child we were blessed with. I read a book about how to choose the sex of your child, and it recommended conceiving earlier in your fertile window if you wanted a girl. This meant that Chris and I had to be specific on timing. Because we were carefully trying, it took us several months to get pregnant using this method. That threw a kink in my plan to have another child in May. My second child was now scheduled to be born January 13.

Since I am a college teacher and coach, I didn't really know how I was going to call in a sub to take over for me for an extended period of time. Not only would the spring semester be starting in January, it was also Daytona season. Who would coach the team? Who would do the extra practices? Who would know what to change, how to plan, and how to make the routine magnificent? I knew who that person was—me.

I was sick nearly the entire nine months, and the only thing that made me feel better was eating. So I did plenty of it. I gained a ton of weight. I had a feeling that I was going to have Ally early. Maybe it was wishful thinking because I was big and miserable. As the Christmas break lingered on and January convocation approached, I started to get nervous. I thought I would have had Ally by now and that we'd get to spend some quality time together before work started back up.

It wasn't happening, so I took things into my own hands—because, as you may have noticed by now, I like being in control. It was a Sunday—the day before convocation—January 9. That morning I took a dose of castor oil, something I had heard brought on labor, and waited anxiously. The only thing exciting that day was making sure I made it to the bathroom on time. Apparently, it's more of a laxative than anything else.

A little disappointed, I went to bed with plans to be back at work the next morning. But maybe the castor oil did the trick after all. As soon as I'd fallen into a deep sleep, a feeling startled me and woke me up. I sat straight up in bed. My water had broken. With Austin, my water also broke, but then it was hours before I had him. This was different, though. I immediately felt intense contractions, and I began to get nervous. My doctor was in Waxahachie, about a forty-five-minute drive from our house. I sensed my time was limited.

We had to call my mother to come over and stay with Austin, and I think she could hear the panic in my voice, because she was there in minutes. Chris and I jumped in the car and took off. We made it to the turnoff to get on the highway to go to Waxahachie and I felt her coming. We'd never make it another forty-five minutes. I told Chris and he turned the opposite way and went to the local hospital. They wheeled me in from the ER entrance and Ally barely waited for the doctor to arrive. She was born less than an hour from the time I woke up. She made her entrance on January 10 in the wee hours of the morning.

That day was convocation at work. I missed it. I never missed work for anything, but I didn't let myself feel guilty. I'd had a baby, for goodness' sake! I was released from the hospital the following day, Tuesday. The next day, with Ally nestled against me in her infant carrier, I was back at the college making copies of my syllabus for a class starting the following week. She came along with me as I returned to teaching a few days later. Luckily, at home I had a lot of help from Chris and my family to make everything work.

A lack of maternity leave is certainly not best for everyone, but for me it was what worked. I knew that if I could get through those next few months, I would have a lot of quality time that summer to spend with the kids. And it paid off. Just three months after giving birth to Ally, I won my first national championship.

The time when my kids were babies was extremely hard not only due to the responsibilities I had at work but also because I'd returned to school to earn my MBA degree. I knew that I wanted to teach other classes at the college beyond cheerleading (I loved teaching developmental math) and to do that I would need my master's. I also thought it would be good to have for when I decided to move into the business field and out of education.

I'm obviously still waiting on that.

I was pregnant with Austin when I started graduate school. I had to commute an hour and a half there and back to go to school. This was back before the internet and before online classes. Luckily, I had my friend Billy Harlan to commute with me. He was the assistant baseball coach here at Navarro and the one who had reached out to me about the cheer job when it opened up. He wanted to get his master's degree in education, so we decided to take turns driving. He still likes to bring up how I had to eat after every class because I was big and pregnant.

One evening when we were commuting, I was driving and came to a yellow light at that crucial moment when you have to decide to stop or go. I decided to go and was pulled over for running a red light. I still say it was yellow when I went through it, but the police officer didn't agree. Billy told me that I should lie and tell the officer that I was in labor. I knew that I would screw that up if I even tried it. The officer came to the window and asked for my license but I had accidentally left it at home. *No problem*, I thought. I handed him the copy of the paper from when I'd gotten it renewed. He asked if the address was correct and I told him that we had recently moved. He left and went back to his car.

As we waited for him to write me what I was certain would be a warning, Billy gave me a hard time for being so honest. The officer came back and handed me not one, not two, but three tickets. Three! I was at a loss for words. Three tickets? He gave me a ticket for running a red light, not having a driver's license on me, and not having the correct address on the missing driver's license. I'm guessing that officer met his ticket quota that month.

Billy and I trudged through the next few years taking a couple of classes a semester until we both finally graduated. I had just found out that I was pregnant with Ally when I attended my graduation ceremony. It had been a long four years. I would work until 5 p.m. every day and leave and go straight to school two days a week. I would be in class for three hours and then head back. I usually got home around 11:30 p.m. I was coaching, which called for long hours, even on weekends. My graduate program required a lot of group projects and presentations. With my newborn, I was running on little sleep.

Those four years were some of the toughest I can recall. But I am nothing if not resilient. Embracing hard work, no matter what the work you're doing—even if it's a high school job, or a day job that isn't what you dreamed you'd be doing—is worthwhile. Work builds confidence, self-sufficiency, and good habits. Now, when things get tough, I get stronger. And wow, did those years make me strong enough to lift a car. They were rewarding, though. I look at my family and my career and I can honestly say it was all worthwhile. I'm still mad about those traffic tickets, though.

20

FIND A TRAINING BUDDY

When I went on a tour at Southern Methodist University with my daughter, the school of business had a little stock market ticker going around and I thought, *Man, I am so jealous of this generation that gets to go to business school with technology.* When I was in college, we didn't even have computers. I had a word processor and I thought it was the best thing ever. For those who don't know what that is: you type in a couple of paragraphs and then you can hit a button and it prints it for you.

One afternoon when I was an undergraduate student at the University of Texas at Austin, I had some homework on a spreadsheet, and I went to the computer lab, because of course I didn't have a computer at that time. I had never even worked with a mouse before, but as I sat down, that's exactly what was sitting there. I looked around to see other people working diligently and moving this little thing around. And I thought, *Okay, this is embarrassing. I don't have a clue what I'm doing.* I didn't want to ask, because I had too much pride. I just watched everybody and figured it out somehow.

I shouldn't have let my pride get in the way. My life would have been easier if I'd gotten help right then. I like to think that I would have asked eventually if I hadn't had success figuring it out on my own. I tell the cheerleaders all the time: Don't be scared to ask questions. Look for support and advice from people you trust. When you're in danger, you realize just how vital it is to have allies.

One day in the midst of the pandemic, I was notified that someone had tweeted to the college that someone was trying to kill me. I went online and looked. Sure enough, a man from Austin who'd seen the Netflix show had gone on a Twitter rant about how he was trying to kill both Chris and me. Then I saw that the threatening man had requested to be my friend on Facebook, and had sent me a message that used his own name in the third person: "[This man's name] was threatening you and your cheerleaders. I can hear and see him in certain ways."

It seemed that the person making the threats and the person warning me of the threats were the same person. I thought about all those horror movies about villains with split personalities.

Chris insisted on driving me to work that day. Fortunately, as a probation director, he knew all the right steps to take. Michael Landers, my athletic director, had been in a meeting with our HR director and our chief of police to discuss the Twitter threat. He came and checked on me all through the day, which made me feel safer, even if he did give me a heart attack each time he knocked on the door. I was on edge, but it was good to know I had smart, concerned people looking out for me. I'm always telling my cheerleaders to look out for one another, and now I was in the position of taking my own advice and letting myself be looked out for.

This wasn't the first strange thing that had happened because of the attention the show has brought. I've gotten weird messages— mostly just your typical creepy-old-man come-ons. Oh, and one viewer wrote to inform me that I was "a psychotic f***ing bitch." I try not to read those. My mantra when it comes to aggressive messages from strangers is: delete, delete, delete. But a threat of death wasn't something I could just delete and forget about.

I'd never received a death threat before. That was a new one. The same day that the threat appeared, a woman posted on Facebook that she was running in the park by Navarro and saw a man sitting in his car. After her second mile, she noticed him get out of his car and go to the bathroom, so she decided to leave because she got a weird vibe. When she looked back, she saw that he was naked and touching himself. When I heard about it, I wondered if it was the same man who was sending the death threats.

ID is required for anyone entering the gym where we practice, and my office locks from the inside, so there should never be an issue, but we realized that we needed to tighten security a bit after the show came out. People were up here every day taking pictures in front of the college, trying to find us. We had to cover all the windows in the gym or else people would be filming our practices. Then one day we were practicing and something strange happened. I was just sitting down watching because our choreographer was working and doing formations and Andy turned around and he said, "No filming, sir."

"Who are you talking to?" I asked.

Andy pointed to a man standing at the back of the gym with a camera pointed at the gym floor. We have closed practices, so no one should ever be doing that.

"Who is that guy?" I said.

"I don't know," Andy replied with a shrug.

I got up and went back there and I said, "Can I help you?"

And he said, "I saw your show and I wanted to come see if I could meet you." He'd driven to Corsicana from Austin, he said. He kind of seemed a little unkempt, a little dirty. He didn't look homeless, just disheveled. He told me he'd worked in the maintenance department at the University of Texas when I was a student there. That freaked me out.

I said, "Oh, you came from Austin to find us?"

And he said, "Yeah, well my daughter was going to be somewhere in another town, so I thought I would come by here."

I said, "Oh, okay, but we have closed practices."

He said, "Can I get a picture?"

I took a picture with him, because I thought then he might leave. And he did leave. We kept on with practice, but as I watched the team work out I kept thinking, *How did that guy get in here?* I found it very unnerving. You can't even get into the gym without a student

ID. After practice, I called our campus police and said, "Hey, this guy came into the gym. I don't know how he got through, but can you tell the front desk not to let anyone in unless they know from me that we're expecting them?"

Campus security pulled the security footage and saw that the lady taking IDs was distracted, so the man went around the line and made it in without being checked.

Two days later, I was in my office, which is located up some stairs in our main gym facility, kind of hidden away. Andy and Morgan were there. We were discussing a recent practice when somebody knocked on the door. Nobody ever comes to my office except cheerleaders so I opened the door expecting to see someone on the team. It was another older man.

"Oh, hi, can I help you?" I said.

And he said the same thing. "I watched your show. I wanted to see if I could get a picture with you."

I didn't feel comfortable having a stranger come into my office, so I turned around and shot Andy and Morgan a meaningful look. They jumped up and we all walked downstairs and took a picture with him and he left.

After that, I told the athletic director, "Hey, this is twice this week that some stranger made his way into the building and made me feel uncomfortable. If someone's looking for me, they need to go to you, okay? And nobody should tell anyone where my office is." He took my concerns seriously and after securing the building he kept checking in on me to make sure I was okay.

It reminded me of something that happened back when I was a college student working at Rick's Hair Salon. I had noticed a guy following me around campus. He started talking to me and asked me where I worked out. The next day he followed me from my campus bus stop to class. It freaked me out. The following week I was cleaning a tanning bed, bent over with my butt in the air. I felt someone's presence and looked up. The guy was standing there right behind me. I was so startled I screamed. My heart was racing as I ran to the front as fast as I could.

Apparently, the man had signed up for a tanning membership in order to get close to me. Rick didn't even need to ask any questions. He looked at my face and saw that I was scared. He gave the guy his money back and made sure that he never came back to the shop again.

It seems obvious now, but it's taken me a long time to become truly aware of how important it is to have people around who are looking out for you. And it's not only safe; it's way more fun to have someone by your side if you're doing something new.

I've always tried to travel with my girlfriends whenever possible. On those first trips to Daytona, I invited my best friends. Louis, my mentor, would call them my "girlfriends support system" and joke that he was our chaperone. And when our daughters were babies, my best friend, Jeri, and I bought an All Star gym together called Corsicana Tumbling Academy (now Corsicana Tumbling Athletics) primarily so we could coach our girls when they were ready. This was a fairly questionable decision from a time-management perspective, as I was already working full-time at Navarro.

And yet we made it work. Some of my best memories are of those trips out of town for competitions with Ally and Jeri and Jeri's daughter, McKenna. McKenna was a year younger than Austin and two years older than Ally, so we were all very close. Jeri and I would drive the three hours to Galveston or wherever we were going while the kids played games in the back seat and goofed off and *every single trip* spilled at least one drink. Jeri and I would be chatting away in the front seats until finally our attention was drawn to the kids, at which point we would look at them and say, in unison, "What *are* y'all doing?"

They were the clumsiest, goofiest, most endearing kids you ever did see. McKenna could get a concussion just walking down the street because she would trip or slip on a patch of ice. After outgrowing that awkwardness, McKenna cheered for me here at Navarro for two years and then she went on and cheered at Texas Tech, where Jeri went, and then Austin went to Texas Tech.

Now that our kids are grown and we sold the gym, we don't talk all day every day, but whenever I need anything, Jeri is the person I call. She would drop anything for anyone. That's just the kind of person she is. It's been so good to have her in my corner, especially in recent years, as I've struggled to take care of my father while working full-time.

Five years ago, my father had a stroke. My sister, Melanie, and I have taken care of him ever since. He still lives at home by himself. The stroke had an effect on his brain. He used to be the authority in our family but now the roles are reversed. I do his finances. Melanie handles the doctor appointments. We took his car away a year ago, so now we take him everywhere. We've even considered assisted living so he could have more of a social life during the day before we stop by in the evenings to take him food or visit. It's been a long five years.

Melanie, a special-education teacher, is older than me by eighteen months, but I've always been the bossy one. We are completely different. We don't look alike. We don't act alike. (She is, to be sure, way nicer than I am.) And yet we've always been very close. She even lives right around the corner from me!

We were actually pretty good kids, considering what kids can get into, but it seemed like anytime we did something we weren't supposed to, we got caught. We were reminiscing the other day about the time I begged (she incorrectly said "forced") our dad to let me drive her brand-new Buick Skylark home from the country club to our house when I was fourteen. My friend and I and Melanie and her friend got in the car. At the wheel, I was chatting away, looking at my audience in the back seat, not paying sufficient attention to the road.

Well, I failed to notice that I was about to cross a set of railroad tracks, and a train was approaching. Everybody started screaming. I stopped before the tracks but not before the crossing gate, which crashed down onto the hood of Melanie's car. I shrieked, threw the car in reverse, floored it . . . and hit the car behind us.

Melanie was hot at me for a long time after that. I did apologize. And I understood why she was reluctant to let me drive the car again, considering that the first thing I did when I got into it was almost get us killed. But we worked through that, as we've worked through countless spats over the years.

What I've learned is that it helps to have a buddy next to you both in the good times—like when Jeri and I drove our girls around—and in the bad times, like now, when Melanie and I are taking care of our dad. I would hate to have been alone for any of that. And it's a lesson I try to impart to my cheerleaders: Train together. Staying motivated, staying safe, caregiving—it all takes a village, let me tell you!

The need for someone by your side was really driven home to me by the death-threat situation. It was such a relief having so many people working to keep me safe. Officers went to the man's home to have a conversation with him about his social media presence. And since he was posting his real address online, he was not hard to find. It turned out he was already known to the police as someone with mental health issues. They didn't believe he was going to act on the threat. Meanwhile, the naked guy near the running track was a different person altogether, and so was the older man who showed up at our practice that time.

What made me feel safe was knowing that so many people had my back. I tell the kids to look out for one another. It turns out that is a useful practice for those of us in charge, too.

21

THE MORE RITUALS,
THE BETTER

hen you go to competition in Daytona, the warm-up area is across the street from the venue. That may seem like a small detail, but if you don't prepare for that walk from the warm-up spot to the performance location, that little detail has the power to completely derail you. I need the team to be 100 percent mentally prepared so they don't get there and say, "Oh! I have to walk all this way? What if that tires me out? We're doomed!"

They must feel confident in every single step they take, so we prepare for the exact number of steps we will need to take. Years ago, I began to incorporate that walk into our preparations. Now in the weeks leading up to Daytona we go through our three mats of warm-up, just like we're going to do when we're down there. We have a stretching mat for eight minutes, a tumbling mat for eight minutes, and then the full big mat for eight minutes. Then they go to the bathroom and get a drink as quickly as they can—and yes, I time that, too.

On campus, to replicate the walk to the venue, they'll walk all the way to the clock tower and then back to the gym. When they get back, they help lift one another over the steps from the ground to the platform entering the gym, symbolizing how they're all going to help each other out to get to the top. It's a cool moment of team building, and we do it every day. Then they go to the back room, as if that's the Daytona backstage, and come out when I signal them.

In these practices, sometimes Andy and I will throw something new at the squad; we'll make them wait longer or for less time and they have to adjust, as they would on the big day. That way, if something happens in Daytona, they'll have been through it already. Because you never know what you might face in competition. If someone were to get hurt on another team and they had to clear the stage for a minute, it would throw off the schedule and our team might have to wait a whole hour and a half after warm-ups to compete. So we run through that possibility as well. If we've done it in practice, then if it happens in Daytona, they'll think, *My body can do that. I know I can do it. It's not a big deal.*

My mentor, Louis, always told me that we had to do whatever it took to keep a team on their toes. He would pull one cheerleader aside before a run-through and say, "Just mess up. Don't warn anyone you're going to do it, but run to the wrong formation and let's see what everyone does."

Then we would watch to see how long it took everyone to figure out something was going wrong and how they recovered. We recorded the rehearsal and showed it back to them so they could see whether or not they'd given away that a mistake had been made.

If the pyramid fell apart because one person ran to the wrong spot, that was a bad sign. We'd tell them, "If that happens, you run right behind her and do the routine from that formation."

Louis would say, "Who knows the routine? You do. Who doesn't know the routine? The judges. If you make a face that shows the judges you've made an error, you're going to get counted off. But if you keep going and keep smiling, a judge might say, 'Well, that was a weird place to put that, but they performed it like it was not a problem, so I guess that was just a creative choice.' Your job is to make it look right no matter what goes wrong."

A lot of our team rituals involve music. I was a big rock fan back in the day: Guns N' Roses, Bon Jovi, that kind of thing. My first concert was seeing Def Leppard outdoors at the Coca-Cola Starplex Amphitheatre in Dallas, now known as the Dos Equis Pavilion.

Being around younger people all the time has exposed me to tons of new music. One of our team's big songs is "See You Again" by Wiz Khalifa. We have a playlist that everyone contributes a song to every year. The kids play the mix when they're walking to the clock tower and back.

We always have one theme song for the year. In 2019, our theme song was "Incredible" by Celine Dion, which is such a perfect song, because it says, "The whole world's watching us now / It's a little intimidating." It's just such a cool song for what we were going through that year. So they play that as they come in and get ready to go onstage.

We probably go overboard on the superstitions. We add more every year. I always pray before I leave the hotel room for competitions. And I throw my underwear away if we lose. Even if it's brand-new underwear—throw it away. Why my underwear? I don't know!

When we're walking together, we have to all go around the same side of every lamppost as a reminder that we need to stay together as a team. Because we spend so much time together, sometimes it's like we have our own secret language.

Every year, the team comes up with a different huddle-break to shout at the end of practice, something that's special to that group. It might just start off as one word and then we'll add a word here or a phrase there. The lines might come from something funny that happened or something strange that someone said. By the end of the season it's a long, weird break that only we completely understand. And it's the break that we do at the end of practice every single day.

Those moments bring us together as a family. At one practice a few years ago I was really mad at the team and I had just yelled at them. Maybe they had done a bad full out or they weren't listening. When I was done with my big, furious speech I said, "Again!" and I pushed play, thinking it was our music. Instead, out of the speakers came a loud rap song. Everybody just fell out laughing.

Even I started laughing, because that song broke the fever. I'd been really angry at them, but I couldn't stay mad when that song came on.

Words are important and mottoes are important. We all need symbols of hope and unity to bring people together. Cheer teams often have letters for their squad and only they know the meaning. The letters for our program are *FIOFMU*. So many viewers have asked me what they mean.

I can't tell you, of course! It's just an acronym that brings everyone who's ever come through Navarro cheer together. I had no idea when we were filming this that so many of these little things would become widely known. I've seen people posting FIOFMU online. At first I was troubled by it. I wanted to shout: "Hey, you can't have those letters unless you're on the team! Those are *our* letters!" But I came to see it as a moving tribute to the team, a form of support.

People underestimate the power of having a shared secret. Having an inside joke or a shared ritual or motto binds a group together. This could work outside of the cheer world. It could be your company's motto or a family joke. Our athletic director, Michael Landers, is very gung-ho about our team mascot. He always says, "It's a great day to be a Bulldog!" He puts that hashtag on everything.

Our longtime former college president, Dr. Richard Sanchez, always used to say, "The best is yet to come." I would always hang on to that: *The best is yet to come.* That phrase has power. Even when we were doing well, he would say, "Yes, things are great! But the best is yet to come!"

These phrases, these rituals, offer us even more comfort in rough times. This past year when the pandemic was changing our world every day, Landers sent around an email saying, "It's *still* a great day to be a Bulldog."

Next year, after the pandemic is over, our rituals will become that much more precise, and we'll be that much better prepared for Florida. FIOFMU!

22

GET OUT OF YOUR
COMFORT ZONE

I n mid-August 2020, I received an email from my agent saying that *Dancing with the Stars* was interested in having me on the show for season twenty-nine. I was thrilled. I have been a fan of *DWTS* since its first season. I love the choreography, the competition, the costumes—all of it. As you know, I've even been inspired to create pyramids from watching. The thought of actually being on the show was a dream come true, but I was scared.

We were only a week away from my new team coming to Navarro for the 2020–21 season. Not only was the new team coming, but we were in the middle of the pandemic. It was going to be a difficult season already, and I wasn't sure that the college president would let me work remotely for what could potentially be almost the entire first semester. And yet, I was always telling my students to take risks. It's essential to try new things—no matter what your age; it helps you broaden your horizons. I can't count the number of times I've counseled my own kids to see opportunities beyond what was familiar. I felt like I had to take my own advice.

The first show would air September 14. All contestants were guaranteed to dance on the fourteenth and the twenty-first. The twenty-first would offer the first possibility of elimination. The finale wasn't until November 23.

It's hard for me to delegate. That's why I always work—I like doing things myself. I just don't feel like anybody's ever going to do it the way I do it—and I *like* the way I do it! Besides, the prospect of meeting the new team and then saying, "See you later!" felt wrong.

And yet, with sports suspended until the spring because of COVID, in some ways it was actually the best possible time for me to leave for a few weeks. This was the first, and I very much hope the only, time with no sports in the fall.

When I got the call, I'd been in quarantine for months, certainly not in a workout-for-*Dancing-with-the-Stars* mode. *The Bachelorette*'s Kaitlyn Bristowe had been announced as a contestant in June. I bet she hadn't spent the summer eating cookies in front of the TV like I had. She'd probably been working out every day. Had I known the show was even a possibility, I would have spent quarantine learning how to dance rather than cleaning out my closets.

But this invite was far bigger than anything else I'd ever been asked to do before. I said to Andy, "I don't know if I should do it or not. It's really terrifying."

He said, "Yeah, but we've done a lot of terrifying things in the past few months and we survived."

"You're right," I said. "We did it. It was fine. We can do it. I can do this. No big deal."

The first step was a Zoom meeting with the executive producers of *DWTS*.

I expressed some of my anxiety to one of the producers and he shook his head. "You're going to be good. This is what you do!"

"Well, I'm a coach, not a cheerleader," I said. "I'm almost fifty. It's been thirty years since I was a cheerleader. I don't have any dance experience."

I shuddered, thinking of flailing around onstage with my boobs and butt hanging out of those skimpy costumes.

"Oh, well," he said, "I guess that would be embarrassing if you were really, *really* bad."

"Don't even say that!" I said. "Don't put that out into the universe! I'm sure it will be okay as long as we don't say stuff like that. I'll just work really hard."

I thought the conversation went well, but for days afterward I waited to hear back from them. When I received the news that I'd been confirmed as one of the contestants, I was excited. And terrified, and exuberant, and panicked, and every other emotion you could imagine. I only had a few days to organize everything at work so I could be gone for somewhere between weeks and months depending on how well I did.

The producers asked me to film a few clips of myself and my family that they could use on the show, and they asked me a million questions about my life. At the same time, I was meeting the new team and holding our first practices, and trying to get Andy and Kailee everything they needed to carry on in my absence.

In the middle of all this, Andy and I were working with an app developer to create a cheer app. The developers were scheduled to fly out in September to film content for it. Thankfully, they were able to make a quick trip to Corsicana the weekend I was leaving. I filmed all day Saturday and Sunday morning before heading to the airport. Then it was time to go to Hollywood.

I flew out to Los Angeles with my son, Austin, the day before the fall semester started. (Chris and Ally would fly out to visit before the second show, and Chris would return for the last two weeks I was there, so I had someone from home with me the whole time.)

DWTS put us up in a two-bedroom apartment across from the Grove shopping complex and gave us a rental car to get around. I had to quarantine for a couple of days before I could take my first COVID test. After that, we were tested every day, Monday through Friday, and were required to wear a face mask at all times except during rehearsals, performances, and interviews.

After my COVID test came back negative, they set up my first meeting with my partner. I wasn't told in advance who it would be because they wanted to get first reactions on camera. But I had an educated guess.

Right before the pandemic, Andy and I had been approached by the tour company Faculty about doing a *Cheer* touring show with Live Nation. In fact, COVID hit just as we were about to film some promo videos and put tickets on sale. When that happened we figured, "Maybe it'll just be a few weeks delayed." Those were more innocent times.

While we were discussing the tour idea, Faculty gave us tickets to the *Dancing with the Stars* live show's Dallas tour date. Backstage, we met some of the cast. Val Chmerkovskiy, one of my favorite professional dancers on the show, came up to me and said he'd want to be my partner on the show if I ever competed. He and I took a photo together and he sent it to the producer. He also posted it on Instagram with this caption:

> *A strong woman leading an extraordinary program of young men and women [to] consistently be at their full potential. Pleasure meeting you @monicaaldama and the entire @navarro_college_cheer squad. All of your students were kind and gracious and I know that is a product of a culture that starts from the top. All the best to you and your program. Hope to see you on #dwts one day soon :)*

I was flattered, but I didn't think much about it until I saw him being interviewed a few weeks later on *People Now*. He said that he loved *Cheer* and believed that it had done for cheerleading what *DWTS* did for ballroom dancing: "When *DWTS* exploded on the scene, before that, no one cared about ballroom dancing at all and all of a sudden we're household names. With them, it's very similar and they're so humble about it."

Then he said that he wanted me to be on the show because "I see, first of all, commitment and discipline. It would be a fresh perspective shift for [Monica] to get some tough love and coaching from me. She's very tough on her students and she does a great job creating her program and I want to do the same for her."

In other words, he wanted me to be his partner because I'm hard on my kids and he wanted to have the opportunity to be hard on me. I heard that as: he wants to kill me! And yet, once I decided to do the show, I hoped he would be my partner. I *wanted* a coach who would push me.

The day we were supposed to meet our coaches, I was filled with anxiety. Unlike so many people who go on the show, I don't come from the performance world. As a cheerleader, I competed at a handful of competitions—but that was thirty years ago. Here I was—no experience, vulnerable—about to embark on a wild ride.

The producers got everything ready while I waited outside the rehearsal studio door. Because of COVID restrictions, this season there would be no one in the rehearsal room except the two dance partners. The producers would be in a different room watching and filming with robotic cameras.

They gave me my cue and I slowly opened the door and stuck my head inside. I saw Val standing there in the middle of the room and ran over to give him a hug. I was thrilled to have him as my partner! We talked for a few minutes and then he jumped right in and showed me a couple of dance steps.

I did the best I could and looked to him to see what he thought.

He did not seem impressed. Oh dear. Well, at least I knew where we stood, and I was prepared to work as hard as I could to change his mind.

The next day we had our first official rehearsal. We were given the foxtrot for our first dance and the song "My Wish" by Rascal Flatts. Walking into the room, I won't lie; I was intimidated. Val had already made it clear he didn't have much faith in my natural ability, and I didn't know any of the terminology of the steps he was going to teach me. I also had a posture problem. In ballroom dancing you need to keep your shoulders down and back, chest forward. My whole life, cheer had trained me to keep my shoulders up to stay tight in a formation. It's a big change for your body to keep those shoulders back all the time.

I realized quickly that it would upset Val when I couldn't remember the choreography. I was trying to be a good student and good listener so I rarely said a word, but the more frustrated he got, the more I would lose confidence and shrink into myself. If I grew passive, that only made Val angrier. He would tell me that my energy was low because of my closed-off body language. If he wasn't happy with me, he would just stop and let go of me mid-dance. I would have to either catch myself or fall. I felt like I was slowly sinking into a dark hole.

I was shocked to find myself feeling so inadequate after just a few days of rehearsal. I've always had tough skin. I thought I could take anything thrown my way. But this was different. I felt like a failure and I saw no way out. I couldn't walk away now. Plus, I'm competitive. I don't quit.

The process was just so different than what I was used to. As a coach, I believe that building confidence in people helps you get the best out of them. I fill my mind with positive mat talk and I fill my personal space with supportive people and upbeat energy. At Navarro, we do a ridiculous amount of reps so no one has to feel rushed or unprepared. Even when things go badly at first, I reassure the team that they are capable and that I believe in them. For me, confidence is the key to success. And yet here I was having the confidence sucked out of me, feeling completely inadequate. It was a shock to my system.

As we approached the first live show, two weeks into the process, tensions between Val and me grew. At one of our last preshow rehearsals, I found myself staring into Val's face and thinking, *Just try to break me. Bring it on. I won't let you.*

As rehearsal was wrapping up, Val asked me if I thought we had any chemistry.

"No," I said.

"Why?" he asked.

"Because it's hard to have chemistry," I said, "when all I want to do is stab you in the face."

I had been holding everything in for two weeks because I wanted to be respectful and just do what I was told. But he'd asked, and so I answered.

He looked shocked. He sat down on the couch. "You could have said a lot of things—that you wanted to kick me in the balls or anything, but *stab me in the face*? That's so *personal*."

We didn't say much more after that and then, with three days to go before the first performance, we went our separate ways for the night.

I felt awful. I sent Val a text and apologized for the words I'd used and for not handling the situation better. I expanded a little more on how I felt and how I was lacking in confidence and could use a tiny bit more encouragement. He thanked me for the apology and said he understood, and the next morning we continued to prepare for the first show.

The next night, we were talking to fellow contestant Jeannie Mai and her partner, Brandon Armstrong, in the parking lot. Val said, "Monica and I had a breakthrough. She said she wanted to stab me in the face." The four of us laughed, and it felt like the fever broke a bit.

The dynamic with Val was the biggest challenge of *DWTS* for me, but I also found the unpredictability of TV to be a real adjustment. I received my schedule for each day via text the night before. On show days, I would get my arrival time, live show time, and press schedule for interviews afterward. I would have interviews and fittings scheduled during the week and rehearsal every day either in the morning, afternoon, or evening.

For someone who has her planner filled out for an entire year in advance, this last-minute situation caused *a lot* of anxiety.

On show days, I wasn't prepared for the long run-up to the live show and found it hard to plan for. As I would quickly learn, show days are long! Your arrival time could be as early as 6 a.m. depending on how many people are dancing and what would be filmed that morning. You start with hair and makeup and then head to the stage to do two run-throughs of your dance. Then it's back to finish hair and makeup, and then there's a full dress rehearsal. Then you have just enough time to get your hair and makeup touched up again before you head back to the stage for the live show.

Los Angeles was largely shut down because of COVID, so it was tough running even basic errands. I did find one nail salon doing manicures in a tent outside. It looked like a war-zone triage area. There was a park across the street from my apartment where I could go to work out. Austin and I went to the beach a couple of times early on. But as time passed, I became fearful of catching the coronavirus. If I did I would have been off the show. Plus, I was just exhausted. Normally, Austin would pick up food and bring it to me, and then I would go to bed early. That was as much of a routine as I could manage.

The season hadn't even begun airing—I'd only been in L.A. for three weeks, including a week of quarantine—and already my time on *Dancing with the Stars* was the hardest thing I'd ever done. I was surprised at how fragile I felt and how much better everyone else seemed to be dealing with the unpredictability and pressure. All I could bring was my work ethic, and I fought each minute to work as hard as I possibly could.

Taking a risk means the reward is not promised. And sometimes focusing on what may be at stake isn't the best way to bring your A game. Most days I would be soaked in sweat at the end of rehearsal—but I told myself that being uncomfortable was making me grow stronger. Still, every dance uses different muscles, so there was never a day my body didn't hurt in a new way. Every week I found it hard to get out of bed in the mornings. My back had been hurting since the first week and I was taking a lot of ibuprofen and acetaminophen just to make it through each day. Soon I also started seeing a physical therapist three times a week. Working out four hours a day, I was definitely in the best shape I'd been in a long, long time. But I didn't know if it would be enough. I told myself that no matter what happened, simply by getting out of my Navarro bubble, I was going to get something out of the experience.

23

WHEN YOU'RE GOING THROUGH HARD TIMES, KEEP GOING

O n the day of the first live show, a production assistant, Corey (whom I adored), came to my trailer early and told me I had five minutes before walking to the stage. I asked why we were going and he said rehearsal. I had no idea we were going to have a rehearsal *before* the dress rehearsal in our costumes, so I hadn't brought workout clothes. I was wearing blue jeans. But it was too late now. I grabbed my dance shoes, ran to the stage, and did my two run-throughs without stretching or warming up.

Then it was time for styling. Watching from home, I had imagined that wearing those gorgeous clothes and having my hair and makeup professionally done would make me feel like a princess. But, as is so often the case, the reality did not match the fantasy. The stylists were pros and all incredibly talented, but I couldn't help feeling deflated by the look they chose for me for the first show. The hairstyle selected for me looked like something out of the 1940s.

The sparkly blue ice-skateresque dress made me feel ancient, and its mesh neckline cut into my neck every time I turned my head. This was not exactly how I imagined my first dance would go.

At the dress rehearsal, three hours before we went live, I was standing onstage, trying to convince myself that the night wouldn't be a total disaster, when the show's executive producer, Deena Katz, came up to me and asked if I had seen the latest headline. I hadn't had time to look at my phone all day. In fact, I had left it back in my trailer. So Deena showed me hers. On her screen was a story about one of the most beloved characters from *Cheer*, Jerry Harris. He was being accused of sex abuse.

My heart almost jumped out of my chest. I felt like I couldn't breathe.

In the years I'd known Jerry, I saw only joy and lightness around him. At every competition he was the most supportive cheerleader for every team there. And I do mean *every* team. A lot of times, you see people just want to go see the higher-level teams in the popular divisions. But Jerry would sit through the level one teams, the level two teams, the level three teams. He would sit there and yell just as loud for those learning cartwheels as he would the older kids doing complicated routines.

All I'd seen was his big heart. Even though he was disappointed when he didn't get on mat, he still wanted to make sure that his voice was heard. He never let his disappointment show. When someone doesn't make mat, there is usually a period of moping, until they say, "I'm over it. Now I'm going to be the best alternate that I can be."

But he didn't sulk once. When it came to supporting people and seeing the best in situations, I considered him a role model. And now I was learning along with the rest of the world that the FBI had raided his home and that he was being accused of something terrible.

The headline Deena showed me that day at *Dancing with the Stars* was about as shocking and horrifying a thing as I could imagine. I told her that I would not be looking at my phone until after the show because the stress of performing on live TV was already more than I could take.

The next few hours are now a blur. I was about to do one of the toughest things I've ever challenged myself to do, and I'd been punched in the gut with devastating news right before showtime. I tried to stay mentally strong and focus on the task at hand but my mind was in a million places. I put on my game face so Val wouldn't see my confusion. I went back to my trailer for a hair and makeup touch-up and then headed back to the stage for the live show. I knew I needed to grab my phone before leaving my trailer so that I could vote for my team after our performance. I was scared to look but I took a quick glance. I had more than a hundred text messages. I looked away, ran back to the stage, and took my spot for the live show.

I was number thirteen out of fifteen to perform that night. I sat upstairs in the balcony for an hour and a half, full of dread as I waited to perform for the first time on live TV. I'd be dancing a foxtrot in front of millions of people as well as a panel of judges whom I found hard to read, whom I knew could be brutal.

My mind was racing back and forth between the choreography and the news about Jerry. If you've ever performed onstage before, you've probably had that strange feeling that pops up right before showtime where you can't remember anything at all. It happens in cheerleading, and I learned it also happens in dance. No matter how many times I did a routine, my nervousness over the live performance added an extra level of anxiety and my mind would go blank. Such times are when you need your muscle memory to kick in; you pray it carries you through the performance.

I looked down at my hands as I stepped onto the stage and saw that they were trembling. When they called our name, I felt a flash of terror. Then there we were under the lights, dancing, and my body remembered each turn even if I didn't. Our performance that night went pretty well, far better than I expected it to given how distracted I was. Derek Hough was always more positive with me than the other judges, Carrie Ann Inaba gave me a deduction for my foot coming off the ground—she called it a lift. We scored nineteen out of thirty, in the middle of the pack, but that was the last thing on my mind.

We did press after the show and one person asked me about Jerry. The *DWTS* PR team deflected and she moved on to another question. I went back to my apartment that night and got into bed. I looked at the headline but couldn't bring myself to read the article. (I still haven't been able to read it.) I lay in bed and a tear rolled down my face. Within minutes, I was in a fetal position, full-on sobbing before I fell asleep.

The next week was rough. Tuesdays, Wednesdays, and Thursdays were spent learning a new routine. I was worn out and just plain sad. That Tuesday TMZ was waiting for me when I left rehearsal. I gave them a straight-arm hand and went directly to my car.

On Thursday I was on my way to a costume fitting when Andy called me to say that Jerry had been arrested. He said that they had released the information from Jerry's questioning. Andy started to read off some of the things that Jerry had reportedly said in the interrogation but I stopped him after a few moments. I didn't want to know the details. I had rehearsal after the fitting and I was already at a breaking point. I love Jerry like my own child. I had never seen anything but love and compassion from him. On top of that, my heart was hurting for the kids affected. I was an emotional wreck.

As I so often do in a crisis, I called Louis and told him how miserable I felt, how much I wanted just to shut down. "Don't lose your spirit," he said. "Don't lose who you are. You and your kids—you are a family. All families have drama. All families know pain."

On social media, I posted a statement, just to make sure everyone knew that the accusations were appalling to me: "My heart is shattered into a million pieces. I am devastated by this shocking, unexpected news. Our children must be protected from abuse and exploitation, and I'm praying hard for the victims & everyone affected. Please respect our privacy as our family mourns during this time."

I wanted to be with my team. I felt they needed me and I certainly needed them. But here I was over a thousand miles away—*dancing*.

I called a meeting that night so we could at least talk virtually. We first met with the whole team to discuss the situation, but there were several people on the new squad who didn't know Jerry at all, so we dismissed them after the first part of the discussion. We then met with the veterans who had cheered with Jerry the year before, some for two or three years. These are kids who loved Jerry like I did. They were his best friends. It felt like we were mourning a death. We held each other up through words of comfort as they wept like I had never seen before.

In the end, I told my team that it had become clear to me that we needed to talk more about sexuality and boundaries. "Look," I said, "my heart can't take another person that I care about ruining their life and hurting other people. All I know at this very moment is that the first thing I can do is work on getting us educated."

I made a plan to bring in people to talk to the team about these issues and to make sure that, in addition to going to class and working hard to do their best job on the team, they were also acting responsibly and with respect for others online and in their personal lives.

I went to bed that night physically and emotionally empty. Thank God I hadn't gone online.

What I have learned after the success of *Cheer* is that for all the wonderful people who will tell you how much you've inspired them, there are plenty of other people who will come for you hard. I didn't believe this before, but now I do: social media is a breeding ground for hate. When I looked at my Instagram account, I saw direct messages and comments below my post with hateful things directed at me because of Jerry's situation.

People seemed to think I must have known what he was doing, that I must have allowed it in some way. Some of the kids who cheered with Jerry even received death threats.

There was nothing positive or uplifting in my life as I entered week two of *DWTS*, and tried to learn how to dance the jive to Taylor Swift's "Shake It Off."

At least the jive was a bright, cheerful dance. It felt more like the type of performances I was used to in cheerleading. The rehearsal studio had windows that overlooked a fancy dog hotel. Anytime I wasn't practicing, I would go and stare out the window in hopes that someone would come out with a dog. Occasionally they would, and for a moment I would watch the animal leaping around goofily and I'd feel a little bit of joy. It was one of the few things I actually looked forward to during those early weeks.

I worried about whether the judges liked me enough. Just the year before Carrie Ann Inaba had told *The Bachelorette*'s Hannah Brown that she danced "like a cheerleader." She didn't mean it as a compliment.

Perhaps it was no surprise, then, that Carrie Ann didn't like our Taylor Swift jive. She said maybe my cheer fans would like it but it was not really dance. I was near the bottom of the leaderboard that week. I wanted to give up. But I thought back to what Louis had said—"Don't lose your spirit"—and I vowed to push through.

Week three was Disney week. We did a Viennese waltz to *The*

Little Mermaid's "Part of Your World." The waltz was not easy for me. I think after the comments the judges gave us for our jive, Val wanted to make sure that each dance would be full of content for that specific style. That meant that there was little "fluff" and plenty of footwork. The waltz already felt like an awkward step for me, and the choreography, along with the change of direction in the steps, added to my anxiety. With only days to learn it and get it in my muscle memory, I was stressed and struggling emotionally.

Trying to rally and looking for inspiration, I found a Christian station on the radio and listened to that as I traveled to and from the studio. I wanted to fill my mind with positivity so I could find the strength to make it through the day. Val was usually ten or fifteen minutes late to rehearsal, so it became my ritual to listen to Lauren Daigle's song "You Say" on repeat while I waited for him. The lyrics are about fighting the voices that say you're not good enough and leaning on your faith to keep going. The song became my daily anthem and it gave me the power I needed to make it through each day. I'd given my team similar advice, but now I had to give it to myself: when you feel like you can't go any farther, sometimes all you can do is keep putting one foot in front of the other.

24

IF YOU'RE STRUGGLING,
DON'T KEEP QUIET

Week three of *DTWS* arrived and I was still having trouble communicating with Val. And just as I had twice before, I found show day particularly stressful. I spent every free second doing the steps. I even had Val going over them with me in the parking lot. I was relieved when we did pretty well in the live show and got our best scores yet.

Week four, we were given a samba to "Party in the USA" by Miley Cyrus. I didn't know much about the samba, but I did know that it involved hip action and bounce. Val had already pointed out my weakness in that regard, so I was intimidated.

As I started learning the choreography, I realized that it wasn't as scary as I'd thought it would be. One day after we had finished learning the entire routine we had a rehearsal at which we did countless full-out run-throughs. I felt myself going through the steps again and again, getting the slightest bit better each time. By the end, we were both covered in sweat. Val actually took off his shirt and wrung it out, leaving a pool of sweat on the floor.

Despite our exhaustion, at this particular rehearsal I laughed more than I had in the weeks leading up to it. This was also the first day that I felt like I was actually having fun.

It had been exhausting and challenging. But on that day when I felt like I got the samba, I could honestly say that I enjoyed myself. I went back to my apartment feeling renewed and hopeful that there would be more good days ahead.

At that fourth live show, we again received our highest scores yet. We went into the elimination round feeling pretty good because we weren't near the bottom of the leaderboard. Our names were called safe and we left the stage, happy. As we were heading back to the balcony, we had to make our way around the stage. We were listening as we walked when something bizarre happened. When Nelly and Daniella Karagach were called safe, Val and I knew there were still three couples onstage. We were trying to see who was out there when Tyra Banks said, "Which means Anne and Keo and Vernon and Peta are at the bottom two."

But there were three couples onstage! Chrishell Stause was still there.

"Oh my God, Tyra messed up," Val said.

"There's actually been an error," Tyra said after a moment's pause. "I'm looking right now and there are three couples. We have to clarify this. Your bottom two couples are Anne and Keo and . . . Monica and Val."

Val and I looked at each other in horror. We were as shocked as anyone in America when Tyra said those words. We stumbled back out onto the stage as everyone looked confused. Tyra said, "There's been an error in our control room but we're making it happen." Behind the scenes, everyone kept saying, "It's live TV!"

We stepped into the circle of light next to Anne Heche and Keo Motsepe's. Our scores were pretty good, so evidently what put us at risk was that we hadn't gotten enough votes from the home audience. The judges all voted to save us, so we stayed, but from that moment on I decided to assume I'd be going home every week so I wouldn't be completely disappointed.

Week five was '80s night. We were dancing a tango to "Tainted Love" by Soft Cell. I thought the tango would be easy for me because it was a more aggressive dance and I knew I could handle the sharp turns. But Val was pushing me on the difficulty level, making sure our dance had the maximum number of steps. He began teaching me the tango by dancing me through three eight-counts. He was leading and I was following as best I could. I was frustrated because I wanted to learn the steps on my own first. I knew that my confidence during the live show depended on me knowing all the steps without Val leading me through them.

I tried to explain that to him but he didn't seem interested. I couldn't quite get the opening down, and I could tell Val was losing patience. As the week progressed, things didn't get much better. By the time Friday rolled around, I would usually have had the dance down, but not this week. I was still struggling and Val was over it.

In the middle of one run-through, he stopped and angrily told me that I had to stop looking down at our feet. His body language and tone communicated pure disgust. My posture was also an issue. It was the last thing on my mind when I was trying to learn the steps and just make it through the routine. But Val would remind me about my posture throughout each dance by shoving my shoulders back into their proper position. When he made those adjustments while angry, I found it harder and harder not to take it personally.

After a few rounds of this, Val had finally had enough and said he needed a break. He left the rehearsal room. I stood there alone, trying to fight back tears and anger. I went back and forth as to whether or not I should tell him how I felt or just continue to stay quiet and let my anxiety and stress build up.

Finally, I decided that I couldn't go another minute without letting him know exactly how I felt. I texted him and told him that I wanted to talk to him but not in front of the cameras. This was not a conversation that I wanted producers to use for dramatic effect. I asked him to meet me in the bathroom. Yes, I realize this was an odd place for a heart-to-heart, but it was the only camera-free place in the building.

In that bathroom, I laid it all out for Val. I told him everything that I had held in, including how he made me feel emotionally and physically. I was tired of him talking down to me and I was even more over him physically shoving my head and shoulders back and forcing my body into crazy positions that only hurt my back more. I cried. I yelled. I cried some more.

He seemed shocked, which surprised me. But he listened.

The next day Val asked me if I thought that I would be doing as well as I was if he hadn't been as tough on me. He said that in the dance culture he's part of, they throw you overboard and you either sink or swim.

I told him that I absolutely would be doing that well—better, actually. I said that he didn't have to treat me like that for me to push myself. I wanted to be the best that I could be and I was willing to practice all day if that was what it took. I left rehearsals and went home to study videos and continue to work on the steps. I hardly ever even sat down for a drink of water in rehearsal. But as it was, I was slowly sinking into a dark hole because my confidence was being worn away.

Our ideas of "tough" were very different. I told Val that he didn't have to throw me overboard—I had already thrown myself over-board weeks ago when I signed on to do something totally foreign to me in front of millions of people every week. Trying to stay with the metaphor, I said I looked at him as my only lifeline—the sailor whose job it was to pull me back onto the ship. Instead, I felt like he was pushing me under and I was drowning.

In the end, it was a great conversation. We both really listened to each other and communicated what we were feeling. That day, things turned around dramatically. Val chose his words more care-fully. He told me when my posture was bad, allowing me to fix it instead of doing it himself. We had a much easier rapport. He was calmer. I was more relaxed. It showed in our dance. We moved together more gracefully, as though we were, at long last, on the same team.

The day of the live show the most amazing thing happened. I glanced at my phone during the chaos of hair, makeup, and rehearsals. My Facebook page was flooded with pictures of people wearing red in support of my performance and asking everyone to vote for me. My sister-in-law, Diane, had come up with the idea of the hashtag #MondaysforMonica. She'd texted a long list of friends asking them to wear red and share pictures of themselves cheering me on. She asked them to share the idea with their friends.

There were billboards around Corsicana with my picture. The schools let the kids wear red on Mondays in support of me. (The Corsicana Independent School District has a school dress code and only certain colors are allowed; red is not one of them, so this was special!) The school district even put my *Dancing with the Stars* hashtag on its website. The college sent out emails, and soon enough there were people all over the U.S. sharing the hashtag and wearing red for me. I was blown away and so humbled by everyone's support. That week, far more connected than we'd ever been, Val and I danced our tango and once again scored well.

Week six was when I felt like I finally hit my stride. Val and I were to dance a rumba to "Have I Told You Lately That I Love You" by Rod Stewart, and for the first time in the entire contest I felt completely ready to take the stage. Rehearsals had been a pleasure. I had fun every single day. Val had completely changed his teaching method, and our partnership was finally solid. I was delighted to be given a gorgeous teal dress made especially for me. It was shimmering and backless with a long slit up one leg, and incredibly flattering. The hairstylist gave my hair beachy waves that I loved.

That week I dedicated my dance to Chris, and in my package I talked about our divorce and remarriage. The background during our dance was to be the Dallas skyline, absolutely gorgeous. I was so excited to do this dance.

My enthusiasm faded somewhat when I found out that the Dallas Cowboys would be playing a Monday night football game and the Dallas channels would be showing the game on ABC even though it was playing on ESPN as well. That meant that my hometown and surrounding areas wouldn't get to see my dance live. It wouldn't air until 1 a.m. I worried that people would forget to vote during the prime-time window, and I was also disappointed that a dance featuring the Dallas skyline wouldn't be seen by those to whom it would matter.

I shouldn't have worried. My hometown came through again. My friends flooded social media, letting people know that even if the Dallas Cowboys were playing, they needed to vote at the appropriate time. Some friends figured out ways to watch the show live on the computer so they could still host watch parties.

Val and I danced our rumba. At the end, as he pulled me across the floor on my toe, we were both smiling from ear to ear.

The judges' feedback was fantastic. Carrie Ann commented that I'd come into my own. Derek said something wise about my remarriage to Chris—that in the course of a life we have many relationships, some of them with the same person. We received our highest scores of the season and ended up in a tie for first place on the leaderboard for the night.

During the elimination round, Jeannie and Brandon were called safe. Then the judges called Val and me safe. I was relieved because, although we were tied for first, there are no guarantees on *DWTS*. Val and I ran toward the back of the stage. As we made the corner, I saw Jeannie and Brandon and started to run to give Jeannie a hug. I have no idea what happened, but somehow I tripped and fell right on my face.

I had huge bruises on my arm and my knee and my toe began bleeding. As Val picked me up off the ground and asked what happened, I started laughing. Here I was in my elegant gown, having just pulled off an incredibly tough rumba on live television in front of six million people. The judges had praised my line and balance. The extra-tough Carrie Ann had said, "Wow!" and told me I was "so refined, so sensual, so in your power—and you were radiant!" And then . . . I fully wiped out trying to hug my friend. *Not so sensual now, are we?* I thought as I looked down at my injuries. I found it hilarious. And I was very glad my balance had abandoned me offstage rather than on.

Being in first place at the end of the night was a great feeling. Because of my coaching background, I live and die by a score sheet. Our high scores were real validation that the work I had put in was worth it. After we did press that night, I went back to my trailer and felt as though a huge weight had been lifted from my shoulders. I was beginning to understand the crazy routine of *DWTS*. Val and I were working well together at last, and I was finally letting the dance technique sink into my body. Maybe I could actually become a great dancer!

That thought put a smile on my face in the dressing room as I changed out of my elegant teal dress. Driving off the studio lot that night, I looked out at Los Angeles and sighed happily. It had been a hard path, but it had been worth it. For the first time, I felt like I belonged.

The next day I headed to the rehearsal studio for week seven. One of the lovely security guys in the parking lot who keep the cast safe from the paparazzi said to me, "Just so y'all know, this is always where people start breaking down. Your body and your mind— you're just spent. So hang in there. You can do it."

"Funny," I said to him, "I feel the best I've felt the whole time!" I could have used that pep talk a couple of weeks earlier, when I'd been at my lowest. Now I felt like all was right with the world.

Val and I had worked out our difficulties. I'd learned—at last— not to care *too* much about the scores, because they often had as much to do with the quality of someone's story that week as they did with how complex a routine was. I'd also developed warm feelings for all the other contestants, especially Jeannie Mai. I didn't really get to know Charles Oakley and Carole Baskin that well, because they were the first two gone, but they were sweet when I did meet them, and so was everyone else.

Week seven was the Halloween-themed Villains Night. Val and I were given a jazz routine to "Fever" by Beyoncé. I was assigned the part of Nurse Ratched from the TV show based on the novel and movie *One Flew Over the Cuckoo's Nest*.

Val was looking forward to the choreography for this piece. I asked him what the judges would be looking for since it was a jazz number. He said that it was more open, that the requirements for jazz weren't specific.

One of the ideas Val had was that I would run a chair over him and slam it down. The problem was that if I was an inch off, I would bruise him. My greatest fear was that one of us would be grievously wounded live onstage. And moves like that felt to me more suited to a burlesque routine or a freestyle dance than to a jazz number. I decided to trust Val, but I was dubious.

And for the life of me I couldn't figure out what facial expressions suited the performance. The other contestants were doing appropriately scary monster faces to go with their characters. Hoping for similar inspiration, I looked at images of Nurse Ratched. I learned that she had just one facial expression, very similar, alas, to my own: resting bitch face.

I guess I can just do that, I thought.

But after the onstage rehearsal, I saw what it looked like onscreen and realized that the face wasn't working. I looked like a zombie—and not a good, high-scoring, creepy zombie. I looked like I was checked out, a blank slate. That's because I couldn't figure out what to do with my face: Was I supposed to be seductive, crazy, angry? I didn't know. And clearly acting is not my forte. Not having any idea what I was even shooting for didn't help.

The day of the live show I felt off. I felt doomed. I knew that this type of dance would be the perfect opportunity for the judges to score me low if they were ready for me to go. I just had this gut feeling—and, boy, was I right.

Val and I performed, and I thought it went as well as it could have, even though I knew the face thing was a problem. Afterward, we stood there panting and waited to hear the feedback from the judges.

Riffing on our song's title, Bruno Tonioli said he hadn't gotten a fever at all. Inside I winced, but outside I tried to stay upbeat and smiled. He also said I stopped moving my arms too soon and didn't fully extend them, as one would with proper jazz arms. That was frustrating: I could have easily extended my arms, as I had just done the week before for the rumba. Carrie Ann said I struck poses that made nice pictures—great for cheerleading but not for jazz. And she said what we were doing wasn't really jazz.

There it was—I knew it! The problem was that there wasn't enough jazz! That was the nagging suspicion I had been dealing with all week.

Does that sound bitter? I'm not! I just have that hang-up about mastering the intricate rules of score sheets. I'd tried all season to adjust to the fact that the scores weren't totally consistent. At the end of the day, I knew it was a reality show that was produced for entertainment. Knowing that should have allowed me to just relax and have fun. But when you put yourself out there, you want to feel like you're on an even playing field, especially given that you have to hear a lot of criticism.

That night, we received the lowest scores of the evening: a 22/30. It wasn't as low as some of those early scores I'd seen. Carole Baskin had gotten an 11/30 for her paso doble to "Eye of the Tiger." But it put us at the bottom of the leaderboard. After the votes from home were tabulated, the bottom two ended up being me and Jeannie. That was devastating, because I didn't want to go home, but I also didn't want her to go home. She was my closest friend there.

The judges were split. Bruno chose to save Jeannie, and Derek chose to save me. At that point it was up to Carrie Ann. I had a feeling Carrie Ann wouldn't choose me. And I was right. She chose Jeannie. I liked Jeannie so much that her getting to stay definitely took the sting out of my losing. Some people on social media said, "Jeannie looked like she wanted to hug Monica, but they wouldn't let her."

Correct. Because of COVID, we were told not to hug the other couples on TV. But as soon as the cameras went off, I picked up Jeannie and hugged her so hard. I feel like we'll always be friends. (And I felt so bad for her when she had to leave the show later due to a medical condition.)

I flew back to Texas feeling like my weeks on the show had been years. My arrival home was bittersweet. I was so happy to see my family, my team, my friends, and my dogs. But as wonderful as those things were, I would have loved to stay and fight for that mirror ball. I had just found my confidence, and I'd made big strides those last few weeks.

I got to fly back to Los Angeles the following month for the finale. All the contestants were there to cheer on the four finalists: Justina Machado, Nelly, Nev Schulman, and Kaitlyn Bristowe. Jenna Johnson Chmerkovskiy (Val's wife) and Nev ended up taking second place to Kaitlyn and her partner, Artem Chigvintsev. Watching the show that night, I realized how grateful I was for my time on *DWTS*. The show was the hardest thing I'd ever done. Still, I would do it all over again in a second.

In those weeks, some of my deepest beliefs about life were confirmed, especially: don't ever be afraid to speak up about a problem. Val was my coach and my teacher, but he was also my partner. He was only going to be as good as I was. At first I didn't speak up because I didn't think it was my place to say anything, to tell him that his coaching methods weren't getting the best out of me. Everyone made such a big deal about the coach being coached that I felt compelled to be the "extra-good student" and just do what I was told. That wasn't fair to me or to him.

Once I actually explained how I felt, Val changed. He became more encouraging. And that made *me* change and become more confident, which made me less prone to doing things he found annoying. I really do believe that there is almost no problem that can't be solved with the right kind of communication. Sometimes there's a learning curve; it can take a while to learn how to talk to a particular person, to make sure they hear you. But whether it's at school or at work, with family or with friends, if you don't speak up when there's a problem, there is almost no chance it will just work itself out.

Val and I always had good conversations outside the studio.

But once I spoke up and we were able to improve how we worked together, our whole relationship blossomed. I began to see him as the remarkable man he is. At last I could fully appreciate him as a teammate and as a teacher. I found him to be so much more than just a professional dancer. He was always educating me on different topics and aspects of culture. He's a musician, an athlete, a producer, a writer, and a poet. He is an old soul with a kind heart. I'm beyond thankful for the friendship we formed.

Although we didn't make it to the finals, I am so grateful for everything that I learned from Val about dancing and about how to talk about coaching with a fellow instructor. We each had to coach a coach during those weeks—no easy task. Perhaps it was inevitable that for a while it was rough. What made it a great experience in the end for both of us was my finally getting up the courage to tell him that I was struggling—and the immense graciousness Val showed by truly listening.

25

TROPHIES SAVE LIVES

My *Dancing with the Stars* experience made me appreciate cheerleading more than ever. *DWTS* was a glitzy dream world. The world of cheer was my true home, and I was happy to be back with my team and my family.

My cheerleaders often tell me that they feel safe with me because I never give up on them. It's true: I will do anything to make things work out for them. And this foundation of trust is essential in building excellence. People need to feel that you care for them in order to give you their best. Then you have to set high expectations. Expect greatness. Lead by example. Show up early and prepared. Focus on work ethic, stamina, and consistency.

There is drama in cheerleading. We are together so many hours of every day. We fight like brothers and sisters. But just like siblings, after we make up we're even closer than we were before. As the routine evolves, so does our group dynamic.

I get when people insist it's "just" a cheerleading championship. It's not a cure for cancer. I get that. But it's not "just" a sport for the kids. This sport that people have for so long liked to joke about offers a path to self-confidence, friendship, and success. When I look at all the trophies in my office, I don't just see victory. I see hundreds of kids who got to feel like winners, who got to have the feeling that they could set goals and then hit them, work hard and then reap the rewards. A trophy is not just a piece of metal. It's way beyond that. It represents the feeling of succeeding in something. One little trophy can save a lot of lives.

I think a lot about what these kids would be doing for these hundreds of hours if they weren't in a gym with me, throwing one another around, doing push-ups and tumbling. Time after time, I see that this commitment to the sport takes these kids out of bad situations. When you don't have goals, you can get lost. You can get depressed. Structure is what keeps you moving forward and fighting to be better.

The kids on my team are so focused on getting better that they want to spend their time practicing, working toward their goals, becoming physically and mentally stronger. The film crew once asked one extra-outgoing cheerleader if he could take them along when he went out to a nightclub. He was an incredible dancer and had such a big personality that they were sure they could get some good footage of him out on the town.

"Oh, I never go out!" he said. "I go to bed early. I have to stay in shape." I've overheard a lot of conversations in which one of my kids is asked to do something dangerous or dumb and then I hear them say, as if it should be obvious: "Oh, I can't do that. I'm a *cheerleader.*"

And those sacrifices pay off. Whether someone accomplishes a new skill they worked for, or we finally hit the pyramid in practice, or we win a trophy at a national competition—each one of these achievements is just one more accomplishment that together add up to a rich experience. And it's a gift that keeps giving. If you've ever been a cheerleader, you know in your bones that if you work hard, good things happen.

This sport has saved my kids' lives and it's saved mine, too. Every day I pinch myself, grateful for the life I'm living. I wanted the world to see what I already knew—how special these kids are, how determined and resilient, and how much they sacrifice.

In the summer of 2020, as I was writing this book, I got a call from Julie, a lovely PR person at Netflix. It was a dark time. COVID-19 cases were on the rise. Unemployment was soaring. The team couldn't get together and we didn't know when anything would go back to normal. Julie had some good news. It looked like the show might receive an Emmy nomination. We did some press leading up to the nominations, though all our fun plans to bring the kids to L.A. for a performance had long since been canceled.

I logged on to my computer at 10:30 a.m. my time so I could watch them announce the nominees live. Leslie Jones was hosting, and she was on fire. She screamed: "Zendaya!!!" "*The Good Place*!!!" "Octavia!!!" She came across with some serious mat-talk energy.

I liked this headline: "Lord, Grant Us the Energy of Leslie Jones Announcing the Emmy Nominations."

She Zoomed with three other stars: Laverne Cox, Josh Gad, and Tatiana Maslany from *Perry Mason*. I watched as they named the nominees for Lead Actor in a Comedy Series, Lead Actress in a Comedy Series, Variety Talk Series, and a few other categories. Then I learned that the awards for all the other categories, including ours, would be announced elsewhere. I clicked on a link to see the list. I didn't really know what I was looking for, so I just started clicking on categories for terms I'd heard, like *unstructured reality program*. I found four categories in which we had been nominated. Four! Amazing!

My family and I had a group text going.

"I think we got four," I wrote to them.

Then I texted Julie at Netflix and said, "We got four nominations?"

She said, "No, y'all got six."

I wrote back, "What?!?"

That recognition felt great. Just like with Daytona: you put all that work into it, and then even though what you receive is essentially a piece of metal, it gives you that wonderful feeling that you've succeeded.

I group-chatted with the team, and I talked to some of the kids. Morgan FaceTimed me. We were disappointed that we couldn't just jet on out there to California and go to parties, but we knew we'd find a way to celebrate.

Already, our lives feel like a constant celebration. The kids are doing commercials. I'm still DM'ing with Paula Abdul. The other day "Straight Up" came on while I was eating at a restaurant with Andy, Gabi, TT Barker, Austin (the one who broke his ankle), and my son Austin. I sent a video to her of us singing along to it at our table and she wrote us right back.

We get calls like this one from a producer at *Ellen*: "Hey, Kendall Jenner's going to be on the show tomorrow. She's a big fan of Morgan, can we fly her out here and surprise her?"

And the next thing you know, Morgan's on a red-eye to L.A. with TT, James Thomas, and Shannon Woolsey, and the following morning Kendall Jenner's wearing a Navarro uniform and the guys are lifting her into the air on TV. Then the kids fly back to Texas the next day so they can make it to practice on time. It's all been pretty unbelievable.

I just got a package in the mail from Netflix with a card that read, "Congratulations on your Emmy nomination!"

The present was a bottle of wine, wineglasses, and a charcuterie board, along with all these little food items. Austin and Ally assembled everything and we had the loveliest little living-room picnic. And we celebrated together as we watched *Cheer* win four Emmys, including the big one: Outstanding Unstructured Reality Program.

When I think about my time as a coach, I reflect on each of the hundreds of kids who have come through the program. I believe most of them got something positive out of the experience, whether they learned how to be responsible or how to work with other people. I saw just about every one of them grow in terms of self-accountability.

I hear from former team members all the time. They could be out of the program for ten years—it doesn't matter. When something good happens, they'll text me or call me to let me know. They tell me because they know that I'm going to be proud of them. I'll remind them of when they started the program as an eighteen-year-old who couldn't make it to class on time, and now look at them: they're running businesses and taking care of patients and having families of their own. They're good citizens, making their communities better day by day, and it was cheerleading that helped teach them what they were capable of.

The 2000 cheer team was just inducted into Navarro's hall of fame. That was the first year we ever won in Daytona. One of the guys on that team is now an amazing entrepreneur in Houston. He still comes to visit us at practices. He says that this program is what gave him structure in his life. I asked him to assemble a Zoom call for the whole 2000 team, and I got to spring the news on everyone together.

Seeing their faces, I was struck by how well they've turned out. They're teachers, executives, parents—and just good people. (They also look way younger than their age. I said, "Wow, y'all look good!")

One of the earliest team members now owns a cheer gym in Houston, and he's a powerful motivational speaker. I like to get on his Facebook Live events and get inspiration.

I get texts all the time from the kids who are still in college, saying, "Hey, I wanted to skip class this morning, but I didn't. I made sure I got up and went because all I could think about is what you would say to me if I didn't go to class."

Others say, "I never missed class in all my years of college because of Monica." Even though they aren't students at Navarro anymore, they still don't want to disappoint me. On some level, I'm their coach for life. I'll always be a voice in their heads trying to get them to do better.

Many of the kids whom I watched go through Navarro have their own children now. One former stunter told me the other day, "Man, it's hard enough to raise one kid. You had twenty at work plus two at home. I don't know how you put up with us!"

"I don't either, y'all," I told him. But I said it with a smile. Honestly, I think I knew, even back when the kids were acting like maniacs, that one day they'd be good citizens out there in the world, raising the next generations, looking back fondly on their cheer years. It's the messages I get like these that make every sacrifice I ever made worthwhile.

Hearing these stories about what a life in cheer has given to people is what keeps me going practice after practice, year after year. Coaching can be a tough job. I do it because I love it and because there is nothing quite like watching someone who's never won anything before holding up that gold trophy in the Daytona sunshine and telling her friends, her parents, the world, and most of all herself: "Look what we did!"

ACKNOWLEDGMENTS

Thanks to my agents at CAA and to Andy McNicol, Margaret Riley King, Sophie Cudd, and everyone else at William Morris Endeavor for bringing me to Gallery Books.

At Gallery, thanks to the inspiring hands-on publisher Jen Bergstrom, my amazing editor Karyn Marcus, publicity director Sally Marvin, editorial director Aimee Bell, associate director of marketing Abby Zidle, assistants Rebecca Strobel and Sara Quaranta, John Vairo and Lisa Litwack from the art department, Natasha Simons, and copyeditor Polly Watson.

A huge thank-you to Ada Calhoun for helping me tell my story so beautifully. You are such a kind soul, and I appreciate your patience with me as I navigated through an ever-changing schedule with many bumps and challenges. You were always a source of calm during my storms, and I appreciate you more than you know.

Thanks to everyone at Navarro College who has supported me over my twenty-six-year journey of successes and failures. Thank you to Dr. Fegan for being a great leader and to Michael Landers for always pushing me to be my best. It's a great day to be a Bulldog!

Thank you to Andy Cosferent for being my sidekick on the wildest ride I have ever taken. You always push me to do hard things, and I will always cherish our friendship and our time coaching together. You are one of the best!

Thanks to Greg Whiteley, Netflix, and everyone who brought *Cheer* to the world. Thank you to Chelsea Yarnell for always being a friend and for pushing me out of my comfort zone.

Thank you to everyone at *Dancing with the Stars* for the most incredible experience of my life. Thank you to Valentin Chmerkovskiy for putting up with me and educating me on history, culture, and dance. Thank you to Jenna Johnson Chmerkovskiy for encouraging me and lifting me up.

Most of all, of course, thanks to Chris, Ally, and Austin. Y'all have always been my biggest cheerleaders, and I could not be successful without you all by my side every step of the way. I love you guys beyond measure.

And thanks to all the generations of cheerleaders I've been lucky enough to coach. You guys inspire me to be a better person and you are my motivation and purpose to work hard every single day. I will forever be grateful.

ABOUT THE AUTHOR

Monica Aldama, an icon in the cheerleading industry, became an overnight sensation after starring in the hit Netflix docuseries *Cheer*, which chronicles her tremendous leadership in building one of the country's most successful cheerleading programs from the ground up. Aldama attended the University of Texas at Austin, where she earned her B.B.A. in Finance, and the University of Texas at Tyler for her M.B.A. She found her calling at Navarro College, where she turned the program into the gold standard for the cheer world. In the past twenty-six years there, she's brought Navarro fourteen National Cheer Association (NCA) Junior College Division National Championships and five Grand National Titles in competition at Daytona Beach. She appeared on season twenty-nine of *Dancing with the Stars*. Her cheerleaders refer to her as "the Queen."